modern
EXOTIC

modern
EXOTIC

Elizabeth Wilhide & Joanna Copestick

Special photography by Verity Welstead

conran
OCTOPUS

First published in 1999 by Conran Octopus
Limited, a part of Octopus Publishing
Group, 2–4 Heron Quays, London E14 4JP
www.conran-octopus.co.uk

The publishers have made every effort to
ensure that all instructions given in this book
are accurate, but cannot accept liability for
any resulting loss or damage, whether direct
or consequential and howsoever arising.

Commissioning editor: Denny Hemming
Managing editor: Helen Ridge
Art editor: Alison Fenton
Stylist for special photography: Cathy Sinker
Picture researcher: Rachel Davies
Production controller: Suzanne Sharpless

A catalogue record for this book is available
from the British Library

ISBN 1 84091 051 8

Printed in China

CONTENTS

POINTS OF
DEPARTURE

POINTS OF DEPARTURE

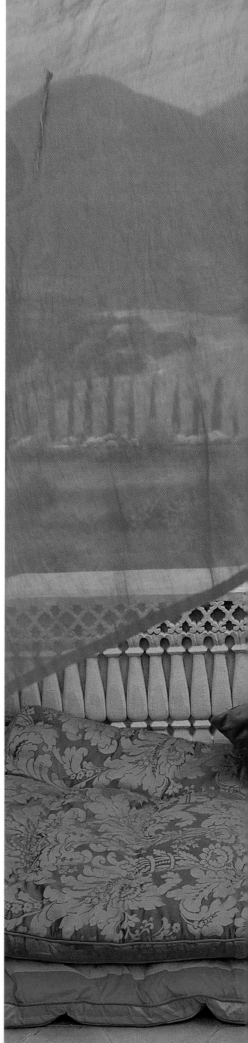

Travel broadens the mind – and our visual frame of reference. As the world shrinks, ideas for decorating are likely to come from sources halfway across the globe, and what were once the exotic souvenirs of a grand tour can now be found by armchair travellers in markets and stores much closer to home.

As with current trends in cooking, music and other creative pursuits, this new approach to decorating is less about reproducing distinctive national styles and more of a vibrant cultural fusion, merging design elements from around the world. The result is an eclectic blend of ingredients and flavours that brings a new sense of vitality to the home.

Spicy palettes of colour, exuberant patterns, earthy materials and original handmade artefacts provide a richness and depth of character. As an antidote to the sheer predictability of mass-market products, the style is anything but dull and uniform. But unlike the cluttered free-for-all of previous incarnations of ethnic style, today's 'fusion' look retains a focused, modern edge. With each

aspect working to create an integrated and harmonious effect, contemporary notions of space, light and comfort are not compromised.

From Mexico to Morocco, India to Indonesia, the sources of inspiration are truly global. African stools carved in dark wenge wood, glittering saris woven through with silver and gold thread, luminous Moorish tilework and the powdery pastels of cotton dhurries add the vigour of colour, texture and pattern to the interior. But the verve and flair these elements bring to daily life is only part of their appeal. Equally persuasive is the fact that such ingredients are often exceptionally economical, and many are available right here at home.

For centuries, ever since regular trading links were established around the world, there has been a creative cross-fertilization of decorative influences. Today, with the accelerating pace of communication, the process has intensified. The exotic look today is a vivid expression of the energy and spirit of that global melting pot.

In the past, ethnic inspiration was frequently displayed in layers of textiles and collections of curiosities from around the globe, an approach that was often more museum-like than home-like. Today, the look goes deeper to create surroundings that are charged with passion and power. A literal interpretation is unnecessary; the creative abstraction of a look – a palette of colours, a suggestion of texture or finish – goes to the heart of the matter and allows personal expression to come into play.

The clean lines of modern rooms make a good foundation for the style, while contemporary design focuses on the basic qualities of light, space, colour and texture. In the modern exotic fusion, the restraint of modernism is tempered and the theatricality of ethnic decorating is given a sharp, new edge. It is the perfect style marriage.

Above *In Rajasthan, India, vivid-coloured cottons are equally appealing whether they are used for saris or as soft furnishings.*

Left *Lush brocades and delicate, filmy muslins provide vivid accents of colour and a sense of luxury.*

Far left *Painting the exteriors of buildings in bold complementary colours is standard practice in Central and South America.*

Left   *Charming in its simplicity, this wall sconce is made completely from natural sources and scrap materials. A gourd has been scraped smooth for the base, while an oval shape and decorative strips have been cut out from a sheet of reflective glass. The candle is held secure in a metal cup that slots into a circular cup hook.*

Right   *Although predominantly Moorish in style, this impressive bath chamber, with its luxurious marble bathtub, includes Victorian elements in the form of the white porcelain basin and wall light. Red terracotta tiles and bricks have been inlaid into a concrete wall, accentuating the high ceiling and decorative arches.*

From India the great trading companies imported entire cargoes of block-printed and painted cottons, the first textiles seen in the West to combine brilliant permanent colour with the ability to be washed. Hugely decorative and appealing, and displaying an incredible degree of finesse, such goods were luxuries of their time and became instantly fashionable, so much so that, in the case of textiles particularly, embargoes were occasionally placed on their importation to protect home-based industries.

Almost from the beginning, however, the decorative traffic was two-way. Eastern producers learned to create designs that would appeal to their new Western customers, or sometimes they were commissioned by traders to copy European patterns, prints or decorations. The result was often charming anomalies – animals, buildings and people depicted by craftsmen thousands of miles away who had never seen them. In the West, too, once approximations of these Eastern techniques were mastered, a whole range of artefacts featured stylized oriental scenes in the same curious hybrid of East and West. Real or authentic, imported or home-grown, chinoiserie took Europe by storm.

Empire-building in the eighteenth and nineteenth centuries served only to heighten the taste for the exotic. The British presence in India – the Raj – together with the French colonization of North Africa and the long-established Dutch links with Indonesia

Right   *Geometric ceramic tiles in blue, green, orange and white provide a vivid backdrop for a lion's head fountain. The sight and sound of running water never fail to metaphorically cool the temperature.*

TRADE WINDS

For Northerners and Westerners, 'exotic' immediately conjures up the remaining two points of the compass. Distant and mysterious, the natural and man-made wonders of the Far East and the South have long exerted a powerful sway on our imaginations. This intense fascination may originally have been based on ignorance, leaving plenty of scope for the imagination to extemporize, but even the cheap flights and mass communication of the modern era have not dispelled the mystique.

Exotic decorating is as old as travellers' tales. Ever since Roman times, spices, silks, porcelain and lacquer have been imported from the East, but it was not until the sixteenth century, long after Marco Polo's largely fictitious account of his 'discovery' of the old Silk Route, that regular trading links between Europe and Asia were established. At that time, the 'mysteries of the Orient' demonstrably lay in knowledge and technique – skills of silk-weaving, dyeing, porcelain-making and lacquering hitherto unknown to Europeans.

From China came lustrous and embroidered silks, fine blue and white porcelain and intricate inlaid or lacquered cabinets.

brought many diverse influences into play. In the Victorian age of stylistic free-for-all, the innate eclecticism of exotic decorating had a particular relevance.

In Britain, exotic imports such as elephant's foot umbrella stands, big game sporting trophies, fringed paisley shawls, elaborate wickerwork chairs, fretted or latticed screens, and a whole range of other ethnic artefacts were added to the *mélange* of trinkets in overcrowded parlours. Whether they were mementoes of a colonial tour, evidence of an amateur interest in anthropology or simply odd curiosities, such elements displayed the Victorian mania for collecting, and provided a powerful expression of the British Empire's dominance in the world at that time.

The decorative influence of the Raj was inextricable from political and economic realities. 'Moorish' style, on the other hand, was less obviously a colonial look, appealing more particularly to the Victorian sense of fantasy. Leighton House in London, with its luminous tiled Arab Hall, was a classic example, but countless country house billiard rooms and smoking rooms – chiefly male domains – were also decorated in a similar mode. The loose informality of cushions piled on divans and ottomans, and layers of Turkish rugs on the floor, generated an ambience of worldly sophistication.

During the eighteenth and nineteenth centuries, industrialization in Britain had begun to pose a significant threat to the trade in handmade textiles from the East. Raw Indian cotton was grist to the satanic mills of the Midlands, where it was woven and printed in imitation of traditional designs. 'Paisley', which was originally a pattern characteristic of hand-woven Kashmiri shawls, takes its name from infinitely inferior machine-made cloth produced in the Scottish town of the same name. With inexpensive imitations readily available at home, trade in authentic textiles and artefacts unsurprisingly dropped off.

However, by the end of the nineteenth century, such ersatz manufacture had succeeded in promoting another great wave of Eastern influence as artists and other progressives became more and more disenchanted with the soulless and often tawdry products spewed out in their thousands by factories and mills. Oriental art, in particular Japanese woodcuts, which reached

Europe for the first time during the late 1850s, was to inspire a whole new decorative and aesthetic style.

Japonaiserie, chinoiserie's successor, was superficially identifiable in many middle-class homes by vases of peacock feathers, spindly bamboo furniture and japanned finishes or lacquerwork, with the Imperial symbol, the sunflower, a pervasive motif. Such fashionable tastes, along with the excessive sensitivities of aesthetes such as Whistler and Wilde, were widely parodied, notably by W S Gilbert in *The Mikado*. But away from the mass market, in more serious circles, the products of both the Near and Far East began to be revered for their authenticity and integrity, qualities also ascribed to medieval craftsmen. The gothic architect William Burges remarked that the Japanese 'appear not only to know all that the middle ages knew but in some respects are beyond them and us as well'. Artists avidly collected blue and white 'Nankin china', as Japanese porcelain was known. Contemporary paintings, such as those by Tissot, show the artistic taste for the exotic in full flight – animal-skin rugs, painted screens, oriental rugs and textiles, as well as the much coveted porcelain.

Arthur Lasenby Liberty, founder of the influential London store that bears his

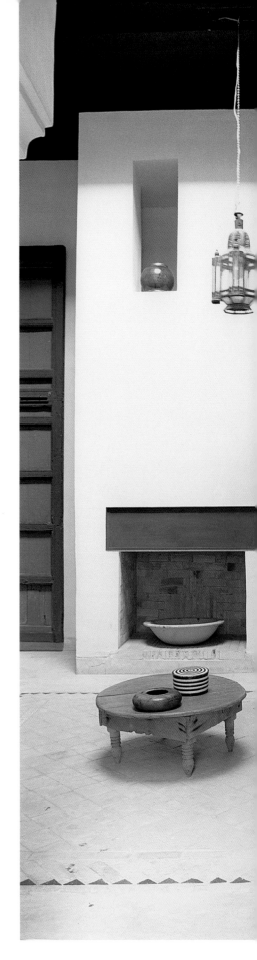

name, was a key figure in popularizing the look. He began by importing coloured Eastern silks and progressed to the marketing of a wide range of goods from Egypt, India, Japan and China: fine oriental rugs, Indian furniture inlaid with ivory and Middle Eastern ceramics. 'Benares metalwork, Lucknow jars, Indian dhurries and Chinese bronzes jostled one another in half the windows of Regent Street,' commented a magazine in 1880. Handmade, idiosyncratic and made of high-quality materials, such products made a powerful contrast to the essentially repro-style of much Victorian manufacture and were instantly fashionable among an artistic and intellectual elite.

To meet the growing demand, Liberty commissioned 'Anglo-Japanese' designs in bamboo and imported furniture from Cairo and Syria: Indian-style occasional tables inlaid with mother-of-pearl, screens and Moorish-style furniture with *musharabeyeh* latticework panels. Like many exotic interiors of the day, such pieces retained a fundamentally European appearance.

The twentieth century has seen its own versions of the look come and go. The louche environment of the turn-of-the-century artist's studio prefigured the rather racy interiors of the Roaring Twenties, with their vivid colour, divans piled high with cushions, animal skin rugs and tinted Chinese lanterns. Africa also joined the East as a source of exotica. Before the First World War, the colonial look – all whitewash,

Above *Exotic does not have to mean ornate. Here, deep blue walls and discreet blinds provide a rich background for simple beds and furniture. A low-hanging, wrought-iron candelabra punctuates the space between the beds.*

Left *Ethnic furniture and lighting are often all that is needed to bring warmth to a sparsely furnished contemporary room. The triangular pattern of green floor tiles inlaid to create a rug effect succeeds in softening a monochrome tiled floor.*

Far left *This wall, punctuated with a tiny peephole window, needs only colour and texture to make its own decorative statement. The large decorative plate and curved-back chair contribute to the overall exotic feel.*

planter's chairs, dark wood and leopard-skin – signalled another take on the style, while modern artists in search of inspiration found the inchoate forms of African masks, carved heads and totems to be powerful points of reference. For North Americans, it was the pre-Columbian art of Mexico, Central and South America, with its stepped ziggurat forms, that provided the necessary stimulus on the immediate doorstep.

But the ethnic style with which most of us are familiar dates from a more recent time. The counter-cultural movements of the 1960s and early 1970s represented its heyday, when hippies, trailing eastwards

in search of spiritual enlightenment, brought back a whole kit bag of ethnic paraphernalia. Embroidered textiles, printed Indian cottons, bronze pots, mirrored and tasselled wall hangings, carved and pierced wooden tables and screens were loosely flung together in darkened rooms that were pungent with the scent of patchouli oil and burning joss sticks. The succeeding generation of global trekkers, travelling the outposts of the world with more obvious political agendas, focused on whatever was indigenous to a region – real, handmade products to act as a counterpoint to the cynical marketing of multinational corporations.

Thus, for Northerners and Westerners, the 'exotic' in decoration has always had something of a subtext. In the seventeenth century, it spelled luxury, mystique and intense desirability, and it is very difficult today to imagine quite the impact that goods such as lacquerwork and porcelain made when they first arrived from the East. The effect was undoubtedly electrifying. For Victorians, the exotic had distinct imperial undertones, mixed with a tantalizing and seductive 'otherness'. In the twentieth century, decorating in an exotic way has often been valued as an expression of protest against established

mores. Through the medium of exotic decorating, each period has found something quite different to say.

The exotic look today is no exception. At the end of the twentieth century, it has finally lost all taints of cultural imperialism. Neither is it particularly synonymous with the luxurious display of arcane skills; it is the primitive we value, rather than the esoteric. Cluttered and unfocused 'hippy' rooms and the self-consciously right-on ethnicism of the early 1970s are completely out of fashion. But the look has taken a new twist to meet the demands of the age. In pared-down contemporary rooms with their free flow of activities, the exotic influence provides the human touch and is evidence of the universal thread of creativity that binds different cultures together.

As the pace of technological change accelerates, as computers and electronic wizardry invade more areas of our lives, exotic decorating has come to represent the lost dimension of handmaking. Exotic, for us, is less a statement of difference and more an expression of continuity and shared human values: the pleasure of vivid colour, the sensual tactility of natural materials, the rhythmic satisfaction of simple patterns and forms. It is an emotional response as much as an aesthetic one, and it speaks to a basic need. In our post-industrial society, which seems to alienate producers and consumers alike, it is a way of restoring soulfulness to our everyday lives.

CREATING THE LOOK

Many of the previous incarnations of the ethnic style of decorating have had something of a period feeling about them. With exotic's strong ties to the eclecticism of the nineteenth-century interior, this is not surprising. The more recent 'hippy' version of the look was similarly associated with a generally retro approach to design that harked back to the early decades of the century, to the sinuous curves of Art Nouveau in particular, while the ethnic styles of the early 1970s coexisted with a renewed interest in all forms of Victoriana.

The modern insight is that exotic can be contemporary. For those who are keen on authenticity, it is worth pointing out that spare, uncluttered, modern rooms are very close in spirit to traditional ethnic interiors, where possessions are often of necessity minimal, and a certain elemental quality of surface and form is at the forefront. Such an emphasis chimes perfectly with the contemporary instinct for light and spacious surroundings where furniture and furnishings have room to breathe.

Exotic decorating in the past has often taken the form of re-creations of distinctive cultural or national styles, however loosely executed. To our eyes, a Victorian Moorish-style smoking room may well remain indelibly Victorian, but the attempt was nevertheless to create a look specific to a particular region. Similarly, japonaiserie often resembled a curious European interpretation of traditional Japanese design, but there was no doubt where the influence came from. In more recent decades, a whole host of styles has appeared in books, magazines and on television programmes, virtually in the form of decorative blueprints to be copied detail by detail in the home. Mexican-style kitchens lead onto Moroccan-style living rooms, Japanese-style bedrooms adjoin Caribbean-style bathrooms: the world in a terraced (row) house.

The exotic look today, however, is less site-specific. A new confidence is emerging that enables us to cast off the security blanket of stylistic labels and devise our own more imaginative fusions of colour, pattern and form. The aim is to achieve a unified look, with everything working together, whatever its origin.

Left   The innate simplicity of oriental decorating has found much favour in the West in recent times. This minimal approach, paired with a deep appreciation of materials, produces calm and controlled interiors.

Far left   This living room is almost colonial in feel, with its tiled floor, white walls, ceiling fan and tropical houseplants.

Below   In a hot climate, an outdoor room is more likely to be a reality than a fantasy. Elegant latticework chairs and a small side table are placed invitingly on a concrete platform flanked by tree-trunk columns. The conical roof, made of rushes, provides all the necessary shade.

Such an approach recognizes that the world is shrinking fast and that achieving an 'authentic' cultural style, given the global cross-currents of influence, is increasingly difficult. In fact, some of the most resonant styles have always been hybrids. What is nominally 'Moroccan' is in reality a blend of African, French and Moorish influences; Mexican style represents a vivid collision between Spanish and Aztec cultures; while the long entanglement of East and West is almost impossible to unravel. Ultimately, it is the fundamental similarities betraying the human instinct for decoration and expression that are perhaps more interesting. We are much better travelled than ever before, and as such are better equipped to spot these connections – the often surprising echoes that can be found between the patterns and artefacts of one culture and another on the opposite side of the world.

Equally important, the modern version of exotic decoration acknowledges the fact that Moroccan or Mexican style can be

faintly ridiculous thousands of miles from its natural surroundings. Recreating a look wholesale betrays, at best, a certain timidity; at worst, it can be almost patronizing, with artefacts displayed like a collection of trophies in a museum. Today, the look does not deny the Western framework, nor does it insist on absolute authenticity. But it does depend on achieving a basic understanding of other cultures so that influences can be translated in a personal and meaningful way. In this context, it is interesting that many of the most successful interpretations of the style have been made by designers transplanted miles from their homeland, drawing on faint childhood memories of particular places they once knew – themes distilled by

time and distance and woven into the fabric of their new lives. In the work of Christian Liaigre, Spencer Fung or Bowles and Linares, the same integration can be seen between modern and primitive approaches to design. Hide-covered stools and tables, hand-forged metalwork, stoneware seats and chunks of unfinished timber marry a purity of form with the evocative power of basic materials.

In creating an exotic look today, you are free to be inspired by whatever takes your fancy, without being driven into the cul-de-sac of cultural pastiche. You can make connections and mix and match decorative elements that might have originated on different continents but nevertheless share a basic affinity. You can remain up-to-date

Above   *Incorporating ethnic elements into period interiors is an elegant way of mixing traditional with modern, ornate with the ordinary. Here, spiralled baskets form a striking graphic arrangement above a formal mantelpiece.*

Left   *No surface is left uncovered in this startling shrine to kitsch decoration. Freehand painting evokes the folk aesthetic.*

Outdoor rooms blur

the boundaries between

indoors and out. Here,

the irresistible charm of

the sea is enhanced still

further with chunky wooden

seating and a dining table

placed, ocean-liner-style,

by the balcony.

and contemporary, but, at the same time, respond to the visceral directness offered by what is simple and handmade.

The look is all about discovering new types of expression within the broadest possible frame of reference. Above all, it is a point of departure, not a destination.

ETHICAL SHOPPING

Exotic decorating highlights the unavoidable issue of ethical shopping. We may be charmed by the idiosyncrasies of handmade artefacts from halfway around the world and thrilled to pay rock-bottom prices for furnishings made of natural materials, but the onus is on us, as consumers, to ensure that such stylish economies are not achieved at the expense of others. The price can be extremely high. The ill-paid labour of underage workers toiling in sweatshops, the destruction of fragile ecosystems or the extinction of endangered species can be the unlovely reality behind the bargain buy on the market stall.

Given the economic disparity between what used to be called the Third World and the West, the low cost of exotic imports remains a significant factor in their appeal. But there is no reason why the gulf should be vast. It is, of course, not always possible to establish the provenance of imported goods, but it is worth going out of one's way to source products from the growing number of retail outlets and suppliers who take care to minimize exploitation. Many of these support and encourage community projects around the world; some even plough a high proportion of their profits back into local development so that traditional skills are kept alive. Training is also provided for local people, and rates and working conditions are above mere subsistence level. In the United States, for example, efforts have been made to restrict the sale of Native American craftwork to reservations, where goods are fairly priced and authenticated by certificate, and those who have produced such work are the direct beneficiaries of the revenues earned.

Such organizations realize that it is in everyone's interest for ancient skills to be preserved, but in no one's ultimate interest if maintaining such skills entails cynical profiteering or the production of tacky souvenirs. Many of the best dealers in exotic furnishings, furniture or artefacts are also deeply knowledgeable about the cultures whose products they market and have links with villages and craftspeople that promote sensible and sustainable exchange.

Similarly, it is up to the global shopper to steer well clear of materials, such as mahogany, teak and ivory, whose continued use poses a serious threat to the environment. The demand for exotic hardwoods has been particularly destructive of natural habitats. In many cases, alternative materials are available, either other species with similar aesthetic qualities or the same wood that has been produced on sustainably managed plantations. In either case, the product should be clearly labelled stating its provenance; if it isn't, don't buy it.

WALLS

WALLS

Exotic decorating relies on a boldness of colour and pattern, the direct use of materials and the unsophisticated vitality of the hand-done effect. The approach is thorough-going, meaning that backgrounds express the same elemental quality as whatever is placed on display. Early modernists decried all forms of ornament, deeming decoration essentially superfluous and dishonest, but the results often proved too sterile to live with. Incorporating exoticism into modernism means creating a tension between a contemporary framework and the basic human impulse to decorate and embellish.

Wall decoration is the keystone of the style. Saturated with colour, inscribed, scored or painted freehand with simple, repeating designs, walls are transformed into rich, glowing surfaces. Rugged plaster, textured papers and natural finishes invite touch, while tiles introduce a luminous quality and the rhythm of pattern.

COLOUR

Over the past few decades, we have tended to treat walls as well-mannered backgrounds. Paint effects may have enjoyed brief periods in fashion, but in most homes walls have remained smooth, plastered, neutral surfaces – the epitome of polite good taste.

Gradually, however, we are becoming a little less shy of allowing colour through the front door. While confirming that off-white

Somewhere along the line, the importance of colour is a lesson we have managed to unlearn. In the past, strong colour was often used in Western decoration, but it was not until the end of the nineteenth century, in the hands of artists and designers such as Whistler and E W Godwin, that colour began to be appreciated for its ability to create mood and atmosphere – to make us feel. It has taken many more years and greater exposure to the palettes of less inhibited cultures to make us see the point.

Colour is pleasure. It conveys exuberance and warmth, spirituality and playfulness, the sheer joy of being alive. Different cultures invest specific colours with their own meanings and associations; colour has always spoken a complicated language of symbolism and tradition. At the same time, different parts of the world have their own instinctive preferences, favoured shades that recur over and over in a wide range of media. In India, where an entire approach to decoration is based on a profound love and understanding of colour, clashing pinks, oranges and reds reverberate; pink, as Diana Vreeland famously wrote, is India's navy blue. Around the Mediterranean, from Greece to North Africa, there is a focus on blue: blue-grey, blue-green, indigo, aquamarine, cerulean – strong, moody shades that make

Above Ethnic motifs and patterns range from strong geometrics to delicate floral designs. Applied to walls, floors and fabrics in equal measure, the effect is both simple and pleasing.

Left Large, bare walls and strong tones combine to create a striking mix. The surface of this intense blue exterior wall has been made even more dynamic with broken colour and texture.

remains the top-selling shade, a recent survey of paint sales has highlighted some surprising runners-up in the form of 'Tuscan' orange and lime green. If colour has increasingly crept into our homes in the last few years, seeing how other cultures handle this essentially life-enhancing element may have had something to do with it.

Let colour loose with a vengeance, ready to cast its spell. In vernacular styles around the world, colour is far from a side issue; decoratively speaking, it is *the* issue, the single most powerful vehicle for creative expression. Where light is strong, colour obviously has extra power, while in areas where daily life is hard and luxuries nonexistent, natural dyes and pigments on walls may be the only means available to create a sense of beauty and joy.

Below Radiating out from the circular window, with its metal grille, the bricks create a subtle but welcome pattern in this plain wall. The complementary green wash on the opposite wall adds extra interest.

and light brown to biscuit and ivory – an elegant sobriety that is enlivened by touches of dull gold and lacquer red.

With the popularity of different national and cultural styles, paint manufacturers have increasingly responded by marketing families of shades pre-selected to deliver the right associations: ready-made Caribbean, Moroccan or Mediterranean palettes to slap straight on the walls. There is nothing wrong about taking the easy way out, and for those who are not particularly confident when it comes to colour-matching, adopting such a scheme at least guarantees a fail-safe result.

Right *Vivid cerulean blue walls as a bold backdrop to an ornate but aged table and a contemporary sofa create a look of faded opulence. The eccentric, sinuous candelabra heightens the informality.*

Above *In La Boca, Buenos Aires, humble materials such as corrugated metal and flimsy wooden trellising are transformed with paint in an attempt to brighten up the basic surroundings.*

Right *Simple stone stairs are discreetly defined with a graphic band of deep blue paint and a thin metal handrail. The rich yellow of the walls and staircase softens the hard surfaces.*

a crisp, graphic counterpoint to whitewashed exteriors and generate a soothing, ethereal atmosphere in the shaded coolness of the indoors. On the shores of the Caribbean, the candy colours of sugar pink, peppermint and baby blue gently weather on sun-drenched clapboard to even softer, more muted tones. But Latin America turns up the volume with the gaudy Mexican palette of lime green, turquoise and hot pink but, most particularly, brilliant blue and canary yellow, creating a carnival clamour indoors and out.

Colour need not be scorchingly bright. The muted, earthy shades of ochre, nut brown and dusky terracotta, graphically set off with matt black and chalky white, conjure up the baking heat of the African sun. The stillness and poise of the Far Eastern interior are echoed in a range of subtle neutrals, ranging from pale green

The problem can arise when little attention is paid to the basic context in which the colours will be used.

It is often said that the bright colours that look so luminous and saturated under conditions of strong southern light do not translate well in northerly latitudes where grey days are more often the norm. There is an element of truth in this: it is fair to say that a certain vibrancy is often missing when the sun is buried behind clouds rather than blazing out of a clear blue sky. But this does not in itself constitute much of an argument for forgoing the pleasure of colour, although it may make a perfectly good excuse for those who have no intention of having strong colours in the first place.

When it comes to using colour externally, doubters may have a point: vivid colours decorating external woodwork and walls can simply look like wishful thinking on a cold winter's day. But indoors it is a different story. It is arguable that interiors in the North and West are better illuminated – by artificial lighting – than their Southern counterparts, where people often go to considerable lengths to screen and shade rooms from bright daylight as a way of keeping them cool. In such surroundings, strong colour sings out and lifts the spirits, whatever the weather is doing outside.

What is important, and perhaps more critical for those in the northern hemisphere, is making sure that the colours you choose suit the setting in which they are employed.

When natural light levels are on the low side, orientation plays an important role. The cooler shades of blue, grey, purple and violet need conditions where the warming rays of a southerly aspect can counteract their innate chilliness. On the other hand, warm, rich colours, from terracotta and pink through to red and magenta, can be used in rooms that do not benefit from much direct sunlight. Colours hovering on the cusp between warm and cool, such as aquamarine, blue-grey and terracotta, are infinitely tolerant and work well almost anywhere.

It is also worth bearing in mind that you do not have to paint all four walls in the same brilliant shade to enjoy the benefits of colour. A single surface picked out in a strong colour makes a vibrant statement of its own. For inspiration, look at the beautifully abstracted decoration in the work of Mexico's most famous architect, Luis Barragán, where clashing planes of colour articulate interior space. Alternatively, you can paint the lower portion of the wall to make a coloured 'dado' effect, using a lighter and less insistent tone above. Simple vernacular houses around the world often lack any other form of

architectural detail, so deep painted 'skirtings' ('baseboards'), 'dados' or 'friezes' also have an authentic look. Similarly, painting niches or alcoves in a resonant shade adds depth and character; shrine-like Mexican alcoves are often painted in a soft matt blue, a colour that is thought to ward off evil.

TYPES OF PAINT

The special quality of much painted decoration in the modern exotic fusion depends on the natural origin of pigments, ingredients as diverse as ores and earth deposits, crushed insect carapaces, roots, berries and plant material of various descriptions. The evocative purplish blue of Morocco, which acquires a luminous intensity at dusk, derives from the indigo plant. Indigo permeates Morocco. The Tuareg, a Moroccan tribe most famous for its fine leatherwork and cloth, are also known as 'blue men' because of the way the indigo dye stains their skin.

The colours derived from such natural sources may appear alarmingly bright but they retain an organic softness that mellows with time and weathering. Their powdery, chalky texture places them in the same bracket as distemper, which was once the universal household paint before modern-day emulsions came on the scene.

In recent years, with the growing desire to use environmentally friendly products in the home, paints containing natural, organic ingredients have been developed, and many of these have similar aesthetic qualities to distemper. Distemper, which can be made to a fairly simple recipe, is also produced by specialist suppliers, although it can be difficult to handle if you are used to the convenience of modern formulations. A more workable alternative is provided by paints with a matt 'distemper-like' finish, available by mail-order or from specialist

outlets. In addition, there are mineral pigments on the market that enable you to make up your own colours.

Standard emulsion paint has little in the way of ecological credentials, but many manufacturers are now producing more vibrant and adventurous shades that would work well in an exotic decorating scheme. Evocative names such as tropical spice, calypso and bamboo will steer you in the right direction. Emulsion also dries fast, hardly smells and provides economical coverage – practical advantages that can be difficult to forgo. A matt finish, particularly if it is well

diluted, has a soft quality that emulates the chalkiness of more traditional recipes.

It can also be worth experimenting with other types of paint if you are after an unusual effect. Dull gold metallic paint will transform a wall into a burnished Eastern background. The new glitter paints add gaudy glamour; a paint that dries to the silky sheen of taffeta is also marketed. In the same vein, there is a 'suede' paint, which is a basic emulsion with an added texturing agent. In natural 'hide' colours of blond, tawny, russet and chocolate, the effect is of sun-baked walls.

Left   Proving that paint can be the main decorative element in a room, deep crimson walls are a warm and enclosing backdrop for a traditional patchwork quilt and Indian prints.

Far left   This ultra contemporary living room is scrupulously simple yet richly exotic, thanks to the blueberry-coloured wall with its textured paint finish. The piece of art on the plain wall contributes to the overall textural richness.

DECORATING WITH PAINT

Unlike other styles of decorating, the emphasis is on vitality, not perfection, and the good news is that wall surfaces do not have to be smooth and pristine. Rather than blow your budget on replastering, which can be expensive, battered walls can be saturated with loose washes of colour to echo the roughcast finishes common in many parts of the world. And the same tolerant attitude extends to the way you execute decorative treatments. Superior levels of skill are definitely not required; in fact, much of the charm relies on an obviously hand-done finish. Neither do you need to invest in any special decorating tools or equipment: improvisation is very much the order of the day.

To enliven all-over colour, apply the paint in thin washes, loosely brushed or rubbed onto the wall with a soft cloth. Build up successive layers in the same fashion to achieve depth and intensity. The patchy, irregular effect will have a textural quality suggestive of old walls. Another broken colour technique that can be very effective in this context is dragging. This consists of nothing more elaborate than drawing a wide brush charged with thinned paint over a base

Above   *Randomly placed spots of green paint cheer up an otherwise plain and uninspiring kitchen wall. The obvious hand-done finish adds to the overall charm.*

Right   *This painted hallway shows how decorative styles can be reinterpreted to suit your surroundings. These brightly coloured geometric motifs, more commonly found in Africa, actually belong to an entranceway in metropolitan Milan.*

colour to leave obvious vertical brushmarks, fine stripes that suggest a woven or grainy finish. Keep the base colour and the dragged top coat close in tone for a subtle effect.

Pattern-making is inevitable, and paint is the ideal medium for making your mark. It is quick, so you have the satisfaction of instant results, and it is relatively easy to undo if you make a mistake. Patterning can be wildly addictive, however, and it is a good idea before you begin to make your patterns to plan exactly where you intend to decorate so you do not get too carried away. A delicate suggestion of pattern is often far

more effective than a rampant wall-to-wall effect. Unlike our rather cluttered Western interpretations of the ethnic look, many true ethnic styles are spare, elegant and minimal, so it is wise to keep a tight rein on your decorative impulses.

Natural sites for wall pattern occur at the edges and margins: along the skirting board (baseboard), at the top of the wall, and at the visually comfortable point about two-thirds of the way down the wall where a dado would be – a point where a change of decorative gear often looks most natural. Alternatively, if you want an all-over pattern,

Above   Painted plasterwork and simple murals do wonders for uneven walls, disguising their worst features but introducing a naive charm to a room. Decorating straight onto a wall means that you have almost immediate results and can rectify any mistakes relatively quickly and easily.

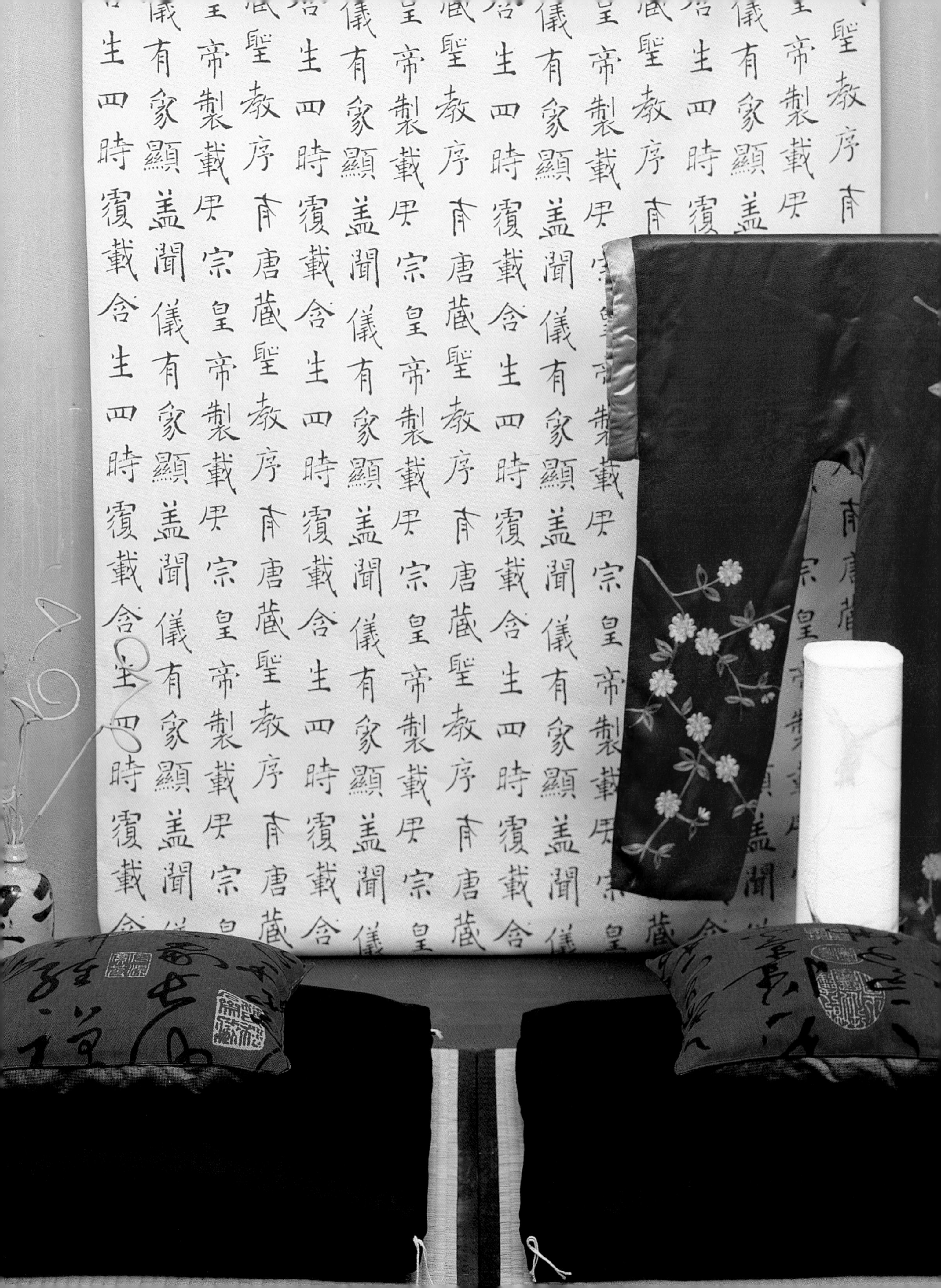

spend some time considering the scale and frequency of a repeat. Small, muted motifs can be closely spaced without becoming too insistent; larger, more figurative designs need plenty of breathing space.

Freehand patterning, the mainstay of vernacular decoration, is well within anyone's scope. There are countless sources of inspiration, from Aboriginal 'dreamtime' designs to African motifs on hut walls, pots, textiles and leatherwork, and amateur anthropologists can have fun spotting the uncanny similarities that exist between different forms of cultural expression, echoes that are woven through the entire fabric of ethnic design. Simple dots, circles, squares, banding with lines and wave-like ripples, peaks, chevrons, triangles ... such basic forms of pattern represent decoration at its most compulsive. There is nothing whimsical or half-hearted about this type of design; added strength comes from touches of gold, vivid colour contrast or the use of graphic black and white. More intricate geometric patterns are a feature of Islamic art: in Islam, attempting to reproduce the real world is forbidden, since perfection is God's alone. Such complex designs require careful planning, a steady hand and a higher degree of skill.

Equally direct and spontaneous is the use of stencilling or stamping to make bold figurative or abstract shapes. Stylized animals occur in much vernacular decoration – creatures such as frogs, lizards, birds and tigers who symbolize certain spiritual

Left   *Wall hangings painted with Japanese calligraphy give an oriental feel to this room.*

Right   *Hieroglyphic-style figures adorn calico banners in a form of restrained wall decoration. Banners are versatile, simple to make and always add visual interest to a room.*

qualities or are believed to possess valuable powers. Animal shapes are widely available in stencil or stamp form, but it is not very difficult to make your own by tracing a simple outline onto a sheet of stencil card or piece of foam rubber and cutting out the shape with a sharp knife. Patterns featuring animals often work well in the form of bands or friezes and in a highly abstracted rather than representational form. Masks, totems, ziggurats and arrowhead shapes are also effective in this context. You might also keep a look out for henna templates, the Indian

stencils used to decorate palms: handprints have a symbolic significance in many cultures as a way of warding off evil.

Calligraphy also makes a dramatic wall pattern, although it takes practice to make confident strokes. Copy characters from foreign language newspapers, but ensure you find someone to translate for you first, or you may emblazon a highly inappropriate message on your walls. For this type of design, the right tools can make a difference. Proper calligraphy brushes and inks will lend a look of authenticity to your work.

PLASTERWORK

Decorative patterns scored, inscribed or
applied to wet plaster have a timeless quality
that painted decoration sometimes lacks.
Another bonus is the textural dimension:
variations in finish invite touch and promote
a comforting sense of being grounded in the
real world. In a sleek modern space, such
tactile experiences add depth and character,
a feeling of continuity to counterpoint the
contemporary mood.

Where walls are made of sun-baked
clay, relief patterning with simple tools could
not be easier. In the West, opportunities to
manipulate raw plaster are necessarily more
limited, but if you are in the process of major
redecoration or rebuilding, it is worth seizing
the opportunity to create more of a three-
dimensional design. In Morocco, walls are
often decorated using the *tadlacht* technique, which consists of adding pigment
directly to the plaster so that colour is literally embedded in the wall surface. The
result, which evocatively unifies colour and
texture, makes good practical sense in a
climate where a painted finish might be
more liable to peel off. A similar effect can
be achieved by rubbing diluted pigment into
undecorated plaster or by mixing pigment
directly into the wet mix. Alternatively, you
can wax a plastered surface and rub the
pigment on top; polishing will bring a low
gloss to the surface. Pigment applied
unevenly to a raw plastered wall has an
appealing patchy look.

For added texture, use a tool to score designs across the wet surface. Repeating even the simplest of marks will have great dramatic impact. Potter's tools are good for pattern-making, but even combs, nails, old kitchen knives or forks can be pressed into service, tracing lines, cross-hatching or gouging shallow indentations into the damp wall. Those marginal or perimeter areas at the top and bottom of the wall are good locations for such embellishment, but all-over effects work just as well.

Alternatively, you can create similar textured effects by embedding materials into the plaster while it is still in a workable state. Sand and sawdust mixed with a little plaster can be applied over a plastered base to simulate stucco or a similar rough-and-ready finish. Small smooth pebbles, shards of tile or glass mosaic, sunk flush with the surface of the wall, add depth of interest and something of a raw organic quality.

These textural effects are naturally heightened if the plasterwork is left more or less undecorated. Standard pink plaster dries to a dusty terracotta, which can be enhanced by sealing it with a matt varnish. It is inadvisable, however, to leave plaster completely raw as the surface will continue to powder and will not be mark- or stain-resistant.

Raw plaster pitted with layers of faded, peeling paint has a charm that no sophisticated paint techniques can replicate. The rich textures have dictated the sympathetic accompaniments of an oval leaf-shaped mirror and a simple clay face.

APPLIED DECORATION

If there is no expanse of fresh plasterwork immediately to hand, walls can be enriched by any number of materials. Some of the most effective of these are small in scale but light-catching: ingredients such as sequins in luminous colours, glass beads with flattened backs, mirror mosaic and practically anything silvery or gilded.

A certain amount of restraint is critical for the success of the final result. Tiny silver sequins sparsely scattered over a deep blue background evoke an atmosphere of Arabian nights; increase the density of the pattern, however, and it becomes more disco nights. With sequins, opt for a vibrant clash with the paintwork – green over warm red, for example – but avoid glorious technicolour.

For the naive charm of vernacular decoration, you might venture further into relief. One highly inspirational and influential example comes from the house of Mexico's most famous painters, Diego Rivera and Frida Kahlo. In a niche in the dining room, a fruit bowl painted onto the wall is filled with a collection of painted and lacquered wooden fruit, glued directly onto the wall. The surreal quality of such decoration derives from the tense juxtaposition of the two-dimensional with the three-dimensional.

Most relief materials can be stuck to the wall using strong proprietary glue; a glue gun can help speed up matters if you are decorating a large surface area. For ceramic pieces, you may need to use a tile adhesive.

WALL COVERINGS

A little distress can be an appealing thing but surfaces that have taken a real beating beg for a cover-up. While wallpaper is the standard cosmetic solution for those who cannot afford to replaster, there are other textured materials that work equally well.

Wallpaper has a long history of standing in for other materials, generally for materials that are expensive and difficult to come by. When chinoiserie was all the rage, papers hand-painted with oriental scenes, fauna and flora stood in for silk hangings. To update the look, opt for papers with a more contemporary Eastern feel, such as grass papers or those that are lightly textured to simulate woven reeds or natural fabrics such as hessian (burlap). If you are not covering a huge area, try large sheets of art paper recycled from plant materials, with fragments of stem, petal and leaf flecking the surface. Again, in a small room, such as a bathroom, newspaper – particularly with foreign calligraphy – can be very effective, as can wrapping paper or interesting exotic graphics. Try Indian film posters for a truly over-the-top 'Bollywood' effect.

Any type of paper can be stuck to the wall with wallpaper paste, but the thinner and more fragile the paper, the more difficult it will be to work with. To protect delicate paper, especially in bathrooms, coat it with varnish. Avoid polyurethane, which yellows with time and exposure to sunlight, and choose a matt acrylic instead.

More overt forms of wall covering range from woven panels to wooden fretwork. 'Dados' of woven palm leaf or thin split cane provide an unbeatable textural dimension, but keep the rest of the decoration suitably elegant and muted. Tongue-and-groove cladding painted a hot, spicy colour, and knocked about a bit to give a weathered appearance, brings to mind the Caribbean, while thin sheets of plywood, with decorative fretwork cut-outs, suggest the gingerbread trim of Latin America.

The classic ethnic backdrop is, of course, fabric. Walls and ceilings swathed in glorious textiles have been a feature of exotically inspired decoration for several centuries, the basic impulse being to recreate the atmosphere of nomadic life. But there are other overtones from a more recent time and these are less sympathetic. The cheap Indian cotton bedspread tacked onto the wall is perhaps more redolent of the student bedsit (dorm-room) than midnight at the oasis. In the modern exotic fusion, it is the quality of the fabric that matters more.

Conspicuous ethnic origin can be too intrusive; concentrate instead on vibrancy of colour and textural interest. A single wall hung with rich fabric can make a more sophisticated statement than a fully tented effect. If your budget is tight, muslin dyed in clashing shades and stapled to the wall makes for exotic minimalism. A staple gun – and more than one pair of hands – are essential tools for this type of decoration.

Left   *In some nomadic communities, particularly in Africa, rugs are used as temporary coverings for upholstery, walls and floors, resulting in a sense of permanency to homes that are constantly relocating. In this cool and informal interior, the same practice has been adopted, offering a cosy evocation of life on the road.*

Above   *Brightly decorated tin cans have been opened out and flattened to form a mock-tiled splashback. Food packaging varies so much around the world that what is an everyday commodity to some is an interesting piece of exotica to others.*

TILING

Tiles are eminently practical. In hard-working areas such as kitchens and bathrooms, where contact with water is unavoidable and hygiene a prime concern, tiled surfaces are easy to maintain and keep clean. Tiling has also long been favoured in hot countries as a way of keeping interiors cool. Aesthetically, tiled surfaces provide an evocative link with lively ethnic traditions. The decorative scope is vast and there is a wide variety of colours, textures, patterns and finishes from which to choose.

Vernacular tiles are a far cry from the mass-produced versions on sale in decorating superstores: bland, anonymous products that are generally as uninspiring as they are uniform. Avoid this by directing attention back to the dynamic and vigorous roots of the craft, exemplified in the handmade and hand-glazed tile, brilliant with extrovert colour and enriched with spirited pattern.

The origins of tile-making lie back in the mists of time. Pottery is prehistoric and is a feature of all civilizations with access to a ready supply of clay, but tile-making itself probably developed in the Near East: thousands of years ago, the Egyptians were known to have used sun-baked bricks glazed in blue for the exterior walls of their houses. With the rise of Islam, Persia became an important centre of tile production, noted especially for its mastery of the lustre technique, or the use of decorative glazes with an iridescent metallic appearance. Tiles in

brilliant blues, greens and yellows were fashioned into intricate geometric designs to adorn palaces and mosques. The Moorish influence subsequently spread around the Mediterranean, informing and initiating tiling traditions in Spain, Portugal, North Africa, Italy – and eventually further afield, to the Spanish colonies of Latin America. At the same time, the quest to replicate the glowing colours of Chinese porcelain also had an effect on the development of tile-making. Islamic tin-glazing, a way of creating sharper and more luminous decoration,

Above   *This bathroom splashback of large, buff-coloured tiles has been enlivened with graphic, African-style motifs, applied in a random pattern.*

Right   *Tiles play a major part in many Mediterranean and North African homes. Simple geometrics, thin borders and a mix of tones in different patterns introduce a sense of unity across a variety of motifs.*

Above *Mosaic panels are not difficult to create, and they look stunning on an otherwise plain wall. This kitchen in an alcove also includes a multi-coloured geometric border around the two work surfaces to create a neat focal point.*

Right *Graphic panels on the walls and floor are contained within ornate tiled borders that complement one another well although they differ slightly in design.*

inspired the development of majolica in fifteenth-century Italy, where a white slip applied over local red clay provided an opaque base for painting and glazing.

In the nineteenth century, Middle Eastern ceramics provided an exotic flavour in Moorish-style rooms. One of William Morris's contemporaries and sometime associate, William De Morgan, was responsible for the revival of lustre. His tiles, where the 'Persian' colours of turquoise, green and black predominate, had a strong influence on Art Nouveau ceramic work.

Some of the more traditionally 'exotic' tile patterns, such as the elaborate Middle Eastern Iznik, inevitably carry a certain amount of historical baggage with them. So, in a contemporary interior, it is often better to focus on simple contrasts of colour, stylized organic patterns or contrasts of texture, as displayed in the basic vernacular tiles of the Mediterranean and Latin America. Encaustic tiles, in which the decoration runs right through the tile rather than just being applied to the surface, are available in evocative contemporary designs. Interspersed with plain-coloured tiles or basic terracotta, such decorative elements add flair and vitality to the modern interior.

It is important to be whole-hearted when it comes to tiled decoration. A splashback only a few rows deep around the bathtub or along the kitchen counter has a meanness of spirit at odds with the robust quality of the material. Take inspiration from the tiled rooms of North Africa, Mexico and South America and extend the tiling at least halfway up the wall.

Mosaic, another ancient art but one with a contemporary edge, also has great potential for creating the right sort of background. Because of the small scale of the individual pieces, it is most practical to work with sheets of mosaic that have been ready-assembled, particularly if you are decorating a large wall surface. Solid moody colour, broken up with random gold, silver or mirror, is particularly effective.

Painted window frame

The patterns, colours and motifs character-istic of traditional Australian Aboriginal art are at once simple and exotic. Their rich muddy tones combine the colours of earth, sand and rock in a palette that is both sooth-ing and easy to live with.

The *pointilliste* painting technique used to frame this bare window is not difficult to achieve, nor does it take long to do as it covers a relatively small area. The technique would work equally well applied along a dado rail or as a painted panel. Before embarking on the painting, it is a good idea to rough out your design on paper first, using images from books on Aboriginal art or exhi-bition catalogues as reference. Better still, go and view some originals.

MATERIALS AND TOOLS
• Tape measure • Pencil • Acrylic paint in four or five different 'earthy' colours • Paintbrushes • Paint palette • Saucer • Sponges • Cotton buds (swabs)

METHOD

1 Decide on the width of border you require around the window and mark it using a tape measure and pencil. Paint on the base colour, then add the basics of your chosen pattern in pencil. Draw around a saucer to form a circle in each corner. Apply the brown paint for each circle with a sponge to create a broken texture.

2 Draw the wiggly lines linking the circles with a pencil first, then paint the lines free-hand using a small paintbrush.

3 Build up a pattern of dots on the circles using cotton buds dipped into individual colours. Start by applying the centre dot in each of the four circles, then work with one colour on all four circles before going on to the next. Finish off by filling in more dots around the wiggly lines. Make sure the cotton bud is damp before loading with paint, and change them regularly.

Stencilled animal border

Inspired by the simple, graphic animal shapes found in African textiles, these turtles, lizards and oval motifs have been used to denote the division of one room from another. They would look equally striking dotted in the corners of a room, along a dado or picture rail, or above an alcove or sink. Single images or clusters of two or three motifs are often more effective than a Noah's Ark-like run of creatures around a room.

The repeating border and animal shapes used here are very easy to make from stencil card; the animal markings are added free-hand with a lighter-toned paint once the stencils have been applied. You can glean ideas for making your own motifs from books on African art and textiles, museums or magazine images. Alternatively, you can buy stencils from craft suppliers.

MATERIALS AND TOOLS

• Pencil • Ruler • Paintbrushes • Masking tape • Acrylic paint in black and a background colour • Stencil card • Craft knife • Cutting mat • Spray adhesive • Stippling brush • Acrylic matt varnish

METHOD

First, mark out the border area using a pencil and ruler. Paint the border in your chosen background colour, protecting areas you do not want painted with masking tape. Rich earth tones lend authenticity to African motifs, so use dark reds, earthy ochres or light tan for a savanna-style background.

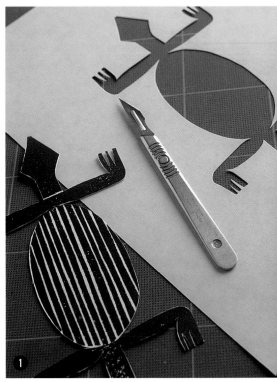

❶ Make your stencils by photocopying selected motifs, or drawing them yourself, to the required size and tracing the images onto stencil card. Cut out the shapes with a sharp blade, such as a craft knife, making sure you work on a cutting mat or other resistant surface.

❷ Fix the repeating border stencil to the wall, at the top of the painted border, with a light coating of spray adhesive. Then, with a stippling brush, colour in the motif with black paint, although any colour darker than the base coat will work well. Move the stencil downwards, lining it up carefully with those stencils you have already painted in to ensure the accurate continuity of the design.

❸ With a stippling brush, colour in the animal stencils in random positions. Paint on any detailing in a different colour using a fine brush. Apply a couple of coats of acrylic matt varnish to protect your work.

Sequinned skirting

The sheer brilliance of Indian colour is an amazing visual treat, giving a sense of the opulent, the exotic and the downright over-the-top, rolled into one fantastic combination of clashing colours. Jubilant, jewel-like tones of fuchsia, tangerine, cobalt and raspberry err on the radiant rather than the romantic, so decorating with such strong colour is not for the faint-hearted. You have to be bold and leave no surface untouched if the mix is going to sing, not sag.

Here, the painted skirting (baseboard) reflects the uncompromising colour saturation elsewhere in the room. Bright pink woodwork is spiced up even more with découpaged and appliquéd motifs, sequins and mirrors in a kitsch mix that is rich with Indian imagery. Use the same decorative treatment elsewhere: on wooden pelmets (valances), doors, freestanding pieces of furniture, even floors. Cut out images from travel brochures as a starting point for

motifs, and visit oriental shops for accessories, fabrics and appropriate furnishings.

MATERIALS AND TOOLS

• Lengths of wooden skirting (baseboard), 23cm (9in) deep • Sandpaper • Paintbrushes • Water-based matt eggshell paint in hot pink • Pencil • Straightedge • Compasses • Paper Buddah motifs • Scissors • Multi-coloured sequins • Tiny mirrors • Wood adhesive • Water-based matt varnish

METHOD

If your existing skirting is quite shallow, remove it and replace with simple beaded skirting that is at least 23cm (9in) deep. Sand back the surface, particularly if it is pitted with years of gloss paint, until you have a smooth, keyed base to work on. Next, apply one or two coats of hot pink paint, either in water-based matt emulsion or quick-dry gloss or eggshell. Leave each coat to dry before applying the next.

❶ Mark out your design over one length of skirting using the straightedge, pencil and compasses. Mark the positions of the main motifs and intermittent decoration on the skirting to ensure you have an even distribution of imagery. Experiment by tacking on a few pieces with removable adhesive to gauge what the finished effect will be. Cut out the paper images.

❷ With a paintbrush apply wood adhesive to each of the main motifs and stick them onto the skirting at the marked points. Leave to dry. For the sequins and miniature mirrors, lay them out in patterns on another surface first to make sure you are happy with the design and sequence of colours. Then, brush on a light coat of wood adhesive to the skirting and attach the pieces.

❸ Once everything is dry, apply a couple of coats of water-based matt varnish to protect the images and toughen the surface.

FLOORS

FLOORS

From the rich colours and intricate patterns
of the oriental carpet to the soothing neutrality of the tatami mat, floor coverings and
treatments provide great scope for expressing an exotic flavour. But perhaps more
significant is the cultural influence of floor-
level living. In the East, there has always
been less emphasis on free-standing furniture such as tables, chairs and beds, and
many everyday activities have taken place in
close proximity to, if not directly in contact
with, the ground. In contemporary design, a
similar shift can be detected downwards,
which only serves to focus attention on the
basic quality of the floor itself.

We are more acutely aware of practical
shortfalls when it comes to flooring than
almost any other aspect of interior decoration and design. Flooring that chips, lifts,
frays, stains, trips you up, or is excessively
noisy, hard or cold is an ever-present source
of irritation and disappointment. The way in
which a floor looks, performs, ages and feels
underfoot are critical factors when it comes
to making your selection.

Although more usually associated with the hard lines of
minimalist contemporary interiors, concrete can provide
a good grounding for exotic decorating. These painted,
interior concrete steps have a pleasingly smooth and cool
surface that contrasts well with the roughly textured,
terracotta-painted plaster walls.

Aesthetically, flooring has a huge impact, which is not surprising since it represents such a large amount of surface area. Increasingly, in modern homes, it is a surface very much on view. As rooms empty out and clutter is banished and the quality of spaciousness is prized above all, the floor becomes an object of unavoidable attention.

A wide range of flooring materials and treatments will fulfil both the aesthetic and practical brief with, perhaps, the exception of wall-to-wall carpeting, which has a tendency to kill an exotic atmosphere stone dead. Narrowing down the options means looking carefully at the overall decorative scheme, as well as assessing everyday requirements and patterns of use.

Choosing the right flooring in the context of this style is a matter of getting the balance right. Where other surfaces are richly decorative, or if furniture is layered with vivid, patterned textiles, basic or neutral flooring can act as a mediating element, helping to preserve the contemporary edge. In a more minimal interpretation of the look, the floor itself can be the means of introducing vitality and ethnic character.

This multi-textured floor, made up of linoleum tiles and vivid blue mosaic tiling, is as visually appealing as it is practical. A discreet under-floor heating system gently follows the contours of the curved walkway, and by incorporating the heating grille into the overall floor design, an additional decorative flourish is achieved.

A graphic herringbone-patterned parquet floor has an added charm when its colour becomes bleached over time. Exotic seating, combined with classic striped curtains and oriental rugs, shows that an eclectic mix of traditional and ethnic furnishings and furniture is not only elegant but also very comfortable.

WOOD

Wooden floors, new or old, are among the most accommodating of surfaces. The integrity of the basic material is reassuring and comfortable; its familiarity has never bred contempt and provides both a valuable connection with the natural world and a feeling of continuity with centuries of tradition. The lively pattern of grain means that wooden floors, however expansive, are never boring or uniform, and they only get better with time, ageing sympathetically with use and care. In practical terms, wooden floors also strike a happy medium. Warmer and more resilient than stone or tile, but not as swathing or deadening as carpet, wood strikes the perfect balance in the flooring spectrum of hard to soft.

In the contemporary idiom, wood flooring has become something of a cliché, the stage on which modern styles of living are acted out. Making a clean sweep of the interior, a wooden floor is the ideal background when there is less in the foreground. In modern rooms with an exotic flavour, pale wood can sometimes strike too Nordic a note. Wood, in any case, is more typically a flooring and building material of the northern and western hemispheres; in hotter or steamier climes, harder and cooler surfaces are often preferred underfoot. Choosing a darker wood or darkening existing floorboards provides a more sympathetic foil. The rich warm tones of tropical hardwoods create a mellow surface, while very dark

In this bedroom, with its decorative African baskets and carved hardwood chair, the exotic flavour has been tempered with pale beech woodstrip flooring. Woodstrip floors are ideal over existing concrete floors or where the floorboards are not in a good enough condition to be sanded.

woods have an elemental quality about them. For a more rustic, Sante Fé-style look, you could opt for American red oak or black walnut. Mahogany, iroko, teak, African walnut, or mutenye, merbau, wenge and jarrah are all exotic species available in various flooring formats, from wood block and parquet to plank and strip. As with all tropical woods, it is important to ensure that the supplier can guarantee their products are either reclaimed or come from sustainably managed plantations.

Many tropical hardwoods are expensive. Cheaper options include woods that have been treated to simulate the dark tones of teak or mahogany. 'Fumed' or smoked beech – beech that has been stained a rich red colour – and smoked oak are among the more successful exotic lookalikes.

If you already have floorboards, darkening the finish is a fairly straightforward process. You will first have to sand off previous seals or finishes to provide a clean and even surface for decoration and then apply

Left   *In the pared-down domestic environments of the Far East, particularly Japan, wooden floors are used for seating as well as for sleeping.*

Right   *Elegant stone steps make an intriguing approach to a narrow, upstairs corridor. A cold, spartan feel is avoided by delineating one wall with square peepholes and painting the other a warming sun yellow.*

CONCRETE

Nothing beats concrete for contemporary edge. The raw brutality of this workhorse material has proved increasingly popular with those who, decoratively speaking, prefer honesty to artifice. Severe, unadorned and about as basic as you can get, concrete is left defiantly on view in many avant-garde interiors, yet the almost primitive nature of the material provides a good grounding for today's modern exotic fusion of styles.

For most people, concrete suggests all that is ugly in the urban environment. But, depending on the treatment of the final finish, it can acquire a stark beauty of its own, with the soft, warm appearance of sandy textures and colours belying its inherent hardness and coldness. In the context of exotic decoration, concrete approximates to the beaten earth floor.

Vivid colour applied to concrete lifts it out of the ordinary. Pigment can be added directly to the concrete mix to preserve the textured finish, or the floor can be covered with acrylic paint and flooring lacquer or special concrete paint. A glossy resin topping is another option. Luis Barragán's contemporary interpretation of traditional Mexican style is a powerful source of inspiration, as are vernacular adobe buildings.

Like plaster, wet concrete also provides great scope for decorative enrichment. Small stones or pebbles can be embedded in the surface to create primitive borders around hearths and thresholds.

a dark wood stain according to the manufacturer's instructions. Top coats of sealant or wax will be required to protect the new finish. Simpler still is to paint the boards a dark woody shade or even black. The glossy lacquered surface of ebonized boards has a distinctly oriental feel.

For floors that can take centre stage, painted decoration adds the uplift of colour and the liveliness of pattern. Wooden floors are easy to decorate. Use either coloured stains, if you wish to preserve the appearance of grain, or standard oil-based paint. If you want thoroughly opaque coverage, try yacht paint, although it is slow-drying and harder to handle. The shock of a solid colour can be enough to suggest an exotic influence. Deep purplish blue, for example, has a Moroccan flair; shocking pink or saffron yellow has more of a Mardi Gras appeal; terracotta, black and white are earthy African shades. Freehand stars, squiggles, chevrons, spots, wiggly lines or similar flights of decorative fancy make evocative painted borders, or you can construct simple all-over geometric patterns of basic stripes or squares.

STONE

Stone is another natural flooring material with a long pedigree of use. Timeless, full of character and at times rather austere, stone adds a sense of grandeur and permanence to the interior. This monumental quality, an association that probably derives from the widespread use of stone in palaces, churches and great houses, works well in interiors where the emphasis is on the elemental and sculptural. At the same time, stone can be defiantly down-to-earth. The rich moody colours of slate are far from cool and stand-offish, while the charming rusticity of randomly sized and shaped flagstones or fieldstones provides a perfect complement to strong primitive decoration.

For those of us living in the northern hemisphere, the greatest disadvantage of stone is its innate chilliness, which, of course, is precisely the quality that has recommended it to those living in hot climates. Stone or tiled floors leading onto stone or tiled courtyards and terraces provide a way of cooling the interior in conditions of extreme heat, and they are easy to sluice down with water to remove dust and dirt. A traditional way of providing natural air conditioning in such areas is to dampen external paving, open windows and doors and let the air cooled by the evaporation of the water flow through the interior.

Without any underfloor heating or an insulating layer of rugs, stone can be uncomfortable in living areas of the Northern home,

which accounts for the fact that its use is more often restricted to hallways, kitchens and bathrooms. Stone is also unforgivingly hard, which means breakages are more common. And it is by no means cheap: it will last many lifetimes, but there is a corresponding investment attached. Most types of stone flooring, except the thinnest 'tiles', should be professionally installed, and you will need to check that the underlying structure can withstand the weight.

If you are looking for a cool aesthetic, limestone fits the bill. Warm, 'flamed' varieties of the stone are available, but most typical are the creamy buff or grey shades, which make an elegantly neutral statement. Limestone is softer than other types of natural stone, which means that it eventually wears down, but such erosion is only evident after decades, if not centuries, of use. For those who like the well-worn look, reclaimed limestone flooring is available, but it is often expensive. New, evenly sized flags or tiles have a crisp contemporary quality. As limestone is a Jurassic rock formation, some varieties display fossilized traces of marine creatures, providing added interest.

Marble is a material that carries a raft of associations, ranging from the tacky glamour of spurious luxury to a more sombre and nobler antiquity. The cool translucence of white marble, graphically contrasted with black marble or slate, makes a classic floor, especially when it is partnered with vividly coloured walls.

Equally evocative are the textured marbles, which are 'tumbled' to provide a soft, matt surface that has the appearance of years of wear. These are available in a range of subtle colours, from off-white through warm red to deep bluish grey.

Whereas stone suggests neutrality, slate is anything but reticent, and although it has seen widespread use in the contemporary interior, it also makes a good foil for more exotic forms of decoration, too. Typical colours are dark and moody: deep blues, grey-greens and charcoals, but more dramatic shades of green, rust, purple and pink are found in varieties imported from Africa and India, veined with coloured minerals and dancing with golden highlights. Texture can also be varied, from smooth polished finishes to riven or rippled surfaces.

Nominally, stone, pebbles and cobbles have a long history of use as flooring materials for both interior and exterior spaces. Elaborate pebbled courtyards are a traditional feature of the Mediterranean and Near East. Set into intricate maze-like or spiral designs, the result is a satisfying blend of found object and primitive pattern. Indoors, pebbled borders around tiles, stone slabs or hearths, or at thresholds, make evocative changes of pace.

For the best overall effect, individual stones should be roughly similar in shape as well as size. They should also be well bedded in mortar to prevent them popping out at a later date.

TILES

Tiles – the poor man's stone – have excellent vernacular credentials. As with wall tiles, handmade or traditional varieties generally score over modern, mass-produced versions when it comes to creating an ethnic look. The essentially rustic character of many of these tiles can, however, undermine a modern aesthetic, but by restricting your choice to solid colours, a more restrained statement can be achieved.

Terracotta tiles create a warm, hospitable floor. They are far less chilly than stone, and the earthy aesthetic works well with Spanish or Latin American-style decoration. Its inherent domesticity particularly suits kitchen locations. Colours range from

Above   *Ceramic floor tiles incorporating stars and diamonds evoke North African motifs, especially when combined with a fretwork chair and sky blue walls.*

Left   *A cool, ceramic-tiled floor, combined with gothic arched windows, soft muslin drapes and a quirky ceiling fan, creates a restful interior.*

pale ochre through to deep red, according to the local clay, and textures can be smooth or rugged. Antique terracotta tiles have a beautiful depth of character. Mexican terracotta tiles, which are made from Saltillo clay, tend to be less durable than their European counterparts. Such floors often look good set off with slate or encaustic tile inserts to provide a graphic contrast.

Other traditional tiled floors also have a role to play. Small squares of black or blue and white tiles have a pronounced North African feel. This type of simple pattern often has the most impact when it is taken

Below   *Tiled floors do not always have to be made from uniform squares. Mixing a range of sizes, planes and colours adds interest and variation when the climate is warm enough to make rugs a luxury rather than a necessity.*

Right   *This hallway, where brown, grey and white terrazzo meets similarly coloured ceramic tiles, is greatly enhanced by generous quantities of natural light flooding through the window and streaming through the glass bricks overhead. A sympathetic combination of tone, texture and materials makes this a hugely welcoming space.*

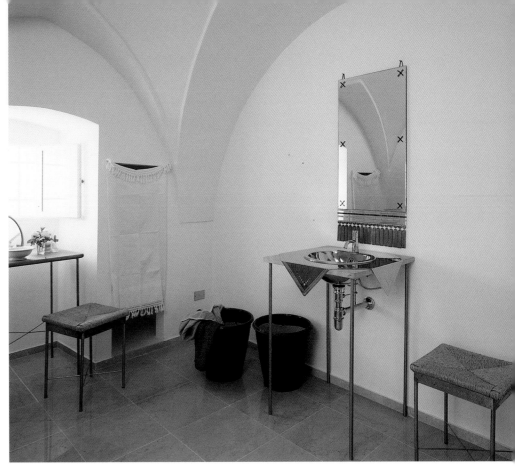

almost to excess, for example, when it extends part of the way up the wall to form a tiled dado. Such an effect can frequently be seen in Mexican houses.

Machine-made ceramic tiles, with their svelte appearance, reinforce strong modern lines. A regular grid of pale ceramic tiles makes a pleasingly neutral background in a contemporary space and creates an atmosphere of coolness appropriate for suggesting a hot country look. Alternatively, opt for a vivid colour to create a spicy mood. Ceramic tiles are available in an enormous range of colours, so it is easy to mix and match with other decorative shades.

With all tiled floors, be aware of certain practical factors. Highly glazed surfaces can become dangerously slippery underfoot, particularly in bathrooms. In such contexts, it is best to choose non-slip finishes.

Marble floors in bathrooms somehow manage to denote both quality and serenity. Gently reflective, they pick up watery shadows and contribute to a feeling of relaxation. In such a clean-lined space as this, with its minimal decorative flourishes, a luxurious surface underfoot is particularly apt.

Above   *Although glass bricks are more often found in modernist homes and reserved for walls and ceilings, here they form part of a floor. Framed with a grid of mosaic tiles, the overall effect is positively Mediterranean.*

Right   *Terrazzo chips are at once exotic and contemporary. In this streamlined kitchen, they provide the perfect punctuation for a simple stone fireplace and splashback. The addition of the rug, with its warm, complementary colours, prevents the room from feeling cold and unwelcoming.*

MOSAIC

While mosaic is often too labour-intensive and expensive to be considered as a covering for a large expanse of floor, as decorative panels or on a small scale in a bathroom or shower stall, for example, it provides a lively flourish of floor-level interest.

There has been a huge upsurge of interest in this ancient art in recent years, and its aesthetic combines perfectly the hard-edged restraint of modernity with more exotic associations. Glittering Byzantine mosaics, with their shimmering touches of gold, are a useful source of reference.

Plain mosaic in a strong colour makes a sympathetic floor covering. But mosaic also has great potential as a vehicle for geometric pattern as well as fully realized pictorial representations. Simple designs are within the scope of the dedicated amateur, but for more elaborate effects it is better to commission a mosaic artist to do the work.

TERRAZZO

Made of marble or granite chips mixed with cement, terrazzo has a surprisingly ancient pedigree, despite its contemporary image. Similar floors have long been common in many parts of the Mediterranean, where the smoothness and coolness underfoot make a valuable contribution to cooling the interior. Today, terrazzo's basic association is with the commercial interior; it is the hardworking but good-looking floor of many stores and public places. In the home, the flecked and colourful surface can be extremely stylish. Terrazzo is either laid in situ or installed as slabs or tiles. It is expensive, as well as heavy, and professional installation is required.

SOFT TILES AND SHEET FLOORING

Modern types of floor covering, such as linoleum, vinyl and rubber, may appear, superficially, to have little of the exotic about them, but in situations where their practical qualities are in high demand, such as

kitchens and bathrooms, they can provide a jolt of colour that is perfectly sympathetic with the style. Linoleum, a natural product, has virtually been reinvented in recent years and is now available in a range of strong shades from midnight blue to rich earthy red, colours that could effectively accompany bolder styles of decoration. The basic ingredients of the linoleum mix, which include chalk and linseed oil, ensure that the colours retain a certain gentleness that mellows with time. Rubber has seen a similar revamp stylistically and comes in a host of electric, vibrant colours. Although the studded or textured varieties have overtones of high tech, the smooth finishes make glossy floors particularly suitable. Vinyl, an oft-despised synthetic material, is widely available in patterns that simulate some other worthier, as well as more expensive,

materials. But solid bright colours are also on the market, as well as heavy-duty vinyls flecked with light-catching quartz to promote slip-resistance. Laid as a swathe of colour or in a vivid patchwork of clashing shades, vinyl is a cheap and cheerful floor for hard-working areas of the home.

All of these materials are available either in sheet or tile form. Choose sheet for an all-over seamless look; tiles are easy for the amateur to lay and can be pieced in bold geometric designs.

Right   A linoleum covering, inlaid with geometric motifs, is both floor and rug. Placed on such a smooth and light-reflective surface, the colonial-style furniture appears much less heavy.

Far right   Soft tiling brings softness and warmth to an otherwise industrial-looking bathroom.

CARPETING

Wall-to-wall carpet, which remains the most popular mainstream flooring, has certain disadvantages when it comes to creating an exotic look. Despite its ubiquity, it retains a strong association with luxury, which works against the primitive elements of the style. Inevitably, it also suggests cooler, more northern climates where an extra degree of warmth is welcome.

Strong colour, again, is one way of counteracting such associations, and shocking shades of purple, magenta and fuchsia that reverberate on the retina may help to banish the suburban image. Close, velvet pile, which has a sumptuous, almost suede-like texture, adds glamour. Alternatively, opt for those relatively new styles of carpet that closely resemble natural fibre floorings: nubbly, textured weaves in various shades of ivory, cream and bone or in elegant greys and browns. A wholly carpeted home is never going to make the most evocative background, but in limited areas the comfort of this softest of all floor coverings may very well be hard to resist.

NATURAL FIBRE COVERINGS

If you like the seamless look of a carpeted interior, prefer the floor to be softer and less draughty than hard surfaces such as stone or tile, but want a more ethnic look, natural fibre coverings may be the answer. Made of different types of plant fibre, these flooring

Above *Natural floor coverings such as sisal, jute and seagrass provide a neutral background for low-key decorating schemes. Softer and warmer underfoot than bare floorboards, they are more 'exotic' than wall-to-wall carpet.*

Right *The bold chocolate and beige zigzags of this carpet are as much a decorative feature in this room as the intricately carved African side table.*

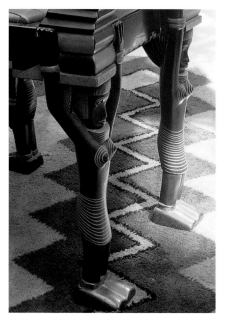

materials combine a classic, modern neutrality with a basic vernacular quality derived from their great textural character. While the availability of natural fibre coverings in easy-to-install, wall-to-wall formats is new and has contributed to their immense popularity in recent years, the origins of such materials go back to ancient times: woven grass or reed matting has long been used as a basic floor covering in many parts of the world. Examples of similar types of flooring were brought back from imperial outposts to grace many country house interiors as long ago as the eighteenth century, while in the nineteenth century, an industry grew up in the Indian state of Kerala to supply export needs.

Today, natural fibre coverings are available in coir, sisal, jute, rush and seagrass, as well as sisal/wool blends. Although each fibre has its own aesthetic and practical characteristics, the family as a whole displays both lively textural interest and, in their natural state, soft, vegetable tones from biscuit to greenish brown. All of the materials are from renewable, sustainable sources. Coir, the coarsest and prickliest variety, comes from the coconut husk; the basic fibre is soaked for months in lagoons so that it becomes soft enough for spinning and weaving. Sisal is derived from a subtropical bush; seagrass is grown in paddy fields; and jute comes from a plant native to India.

Weaves vary from bouclé, basketweave and herringbone to tightly ribbed designs, and colours can also be introduced in the weft strings, adding to graphic impact. Sisal, in particular, lends itself to dyeing and is available in a range of strong solid shades. Seagrass, however, is impermeable and therefore cannot be dyed. In terms of comfort, jute is the softest of all the natural fibres, but it also wears quite rapidly so is best restricted to areas of light traffic, such as bedrooms. Coir and seagrass are much tougher, but can be hazardous on the stairs. Only seagrass is stain-resistant; even with stain-inhibiting treatments, the other fibres do have a tendency to mark.

Natural fibre coverings make discreet and muted backgrounds but, unlike wool carpeting, the overt textural element means that there is never any danger of blandness. In a sparsely furnished Eastern interior, such flooring suggests the tatami, or woven reed, matting that is typical of traditional Japanese houses. There, the standard dimensions of the tatami mat are used as a module for the disposition of interior space with a consequent gridded look to the flooring. In a Western interior, this association can be strengthened by bordering the floor with a graphic banding of dark stained wood or woven jute tape.

Although the new wall-to-wall format has been responsible for the increased popularity of these natural fibre coverings, all remain available in the form of room-sized loose matting as well. Other plant fibres, such as palm leaf, are also made into beautifully textured matting.

Sisal is the easiest natural fibre covering to dye and can be found in a range of interesting colours and patterns. The Moorish-style design of the flooring in this hallway, combined with the tropical plants, gives the space an overall exotic feel.

RUGS

Rugs and loose carpets are the quintessential floor covering in the modern exotic fusion. The rich colours and intricate patterns of hand-woven and knotted rugs from the Near and Far East have been a feature of many previous incarnations of ethnic decoration over the years; today, the scope has widened to include the vibrant, forthright designs of Latin America and Africa.

In the contemporary home, rugs introduce a domesticating layer of comfort that softens strong lines and bold, graphic forms. They manage to combine strong colour with traditional or primitive patterning to act as a focus of decorative interest. A beautiful rug, in fact, can be the foundation for the decorative treatment of a room, suggesting combinations of colours or designs to echo on other surfaces.

Above   *In true nomadic style, oriental rugs double as wall hangings and curtains, their patterns echoing those on the floor rug. Swathes of muslin divide the arched entrance from the bedroom, softening the overall appearance of the space.*

Left   *The strong lines and right angles in the living room of designer Spencer Fung's London home are offset by a richly patterned oriental rug to bring softness, warmth and colour to a contemporary interior.*

Far left   *Rugs are often used as softening devices in spaces where hard flooring can dominate. They also help delineate seating areas.*

Knotted carpets have been made in the Near East since about 1000 BC. When trading links between East and West became established, such textiles were popular imports, although they were not originally used as floor coverings but more typically were hung on the wall or draped over a table.

Carpet-making achieved the status of a fine art in sixteenth- to eighteenth-century Persia, with rugs displaying a panoply of glowing colours fashioned into detailed and often symbolic patterns, such as stylized representations of the tree of life or Garden of Eden. The finest and densest carpets of all might have had as many as a thousand knots per square inch. Chinese rugs, the most luxurious of which were made of silk, have also long been prized. They are often distinguished by light, pretty colours and relief patterns where the pile has been cut shorter around the outlines of designs. Tibetan rugs, often hand-knotted, can be very expensive and tend to display a Chinese influence.

With industrialization and the advent of chemical dyes, cheaper and less skilful imitations of traditional rugs and carpets began to flood the market. Only in relatively recent times has there been a move to return to the old handmaking skills and encourage the use of natural colours derived from vegetable, animal and mineral sources.

Up until this century, exotic rugs and carpets invariably meant those with an oriental or Middle Eastern provenance. Tent rugs, made by nomadic people, were layered in artistic Victorian rooms to suggest the free-spirited wanderings of the caravanserai; more typically, the family heirloom of an oriental rug, or a mass-produced simulation, came to be an almost generic component of the genteel interior. This history of use means that today even fine Eastern carpets can seem curiously lacking in exotic flavour.

Today, the focus has shifted to the more primitive examples of the carpet-making art: bold, forthright designs that display almost an abstraction of pattern. Into this category fall many types of flat-weave carpet, such as kelims and dhurries. Dhurries are flat-weave and generally cotton carpets from India; kelims are made by nomadic peoples in the Middle East, from Afghanistan to Turkey and down into North Africa, and are usually woollen. In both cases, a certain amount of cultural exchange has taken place between makers and importers, with designers and retailers commissioning patterns and colours that are more likely to appeal to their Western customers. In some cases, this has usefully led to the revival of traditional skills and the reintroduction of beautifully luminous natural dyes.

Native American and Latin American textiles also display an intensity of colour and simplicity of pattern. Serapes are thin, flat-weave rugs or blankets from Mexico, which are typically striped in searing rainbow shades. Navajo and Pueblo rugs are equally graphic, with strong contrasts of red, black and cream predominating.

In this quintessential
Mexican interior, where
colour is the dominant
decorating force, the
plain tiled floor is partly
disguised with a rainbow-
hued, flat-weave rug,
introducing even more
colour into the room.

Painted concrete floor

Reminiscent of the Caribbean, these vivid sherbet tones of aqua, jewel blue and saturated yellow are a sure way of cheering up any room, making a focal point of the floor and focusing attention on colour underfoot, rather than texture. A painted concrete floor is both bright and practical. Once sealed with flooring lacquer (clear varnish), it is also waterproof and fairly robust.

The concrete must be smooth before you start painting. If the surface is bumpy or very worn, have the floor screeded by a professional first, then treat it with a coat of sealant to which paint will adhere. The same painting technique used here also works well on wooden floorboards, provided they are sanded back to provide a keyed surface.

When painting directly onto a floor, use masking tape to protect existing paintwork on skirtings (baseboards) and doorways. This geometric pattern was drawn freehand, but you could make your own stencils (see the tiled worktop project on pages 114–15 and the stencilled animal border on pages 40–1) or simply mask out a pattern.

MATERIALS AND TOOLS

• Concrete floor sealant • White matt acrylic primer • Soft pencil, ruler and tape measure • Water-based acrylic paint in three vivid colours and white • 6.5cm (2½in) paintbrush • 4cm (1½in) paintbrush • 12mm (½in) square-cut sable paintbrush for fine details • Water-based flooring lacquer (clear varnish)

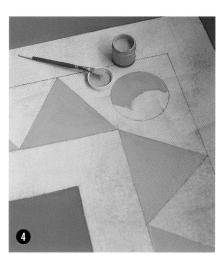

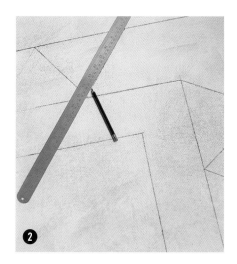

METHOD

First, calculate the floor measurements, then design a pattern on paper and decide on your colours – two or three colours create a better dramatic effect than a multi-coloured combination. If necessary, have the floor properly screeded, then apply concrete floor sealant, following the manufacturer's instructions.

❶ With a 6.5cm (2½in) paintbrush, apply a coat of white matt acrylic primer, which has been watered down in a ratio of approximately two parts paint to one part water, over the entire floor area to be painted.

❷ Using a soft pencil, ruler and tape measure, mark out your chosen design carefully on the floor.

❸ Fill in the pattern with the acrylic paints, starting with the predominant colour – here, the blue – using a 6.5cm (2½in) brush.

❹ Use a 4cm (1½in) paintbrush, and a square-cut sable brush for the finer details, to fill in the other colours. Allow each coat of paint to dry before applying the second coat, and work with one colour at a time. Once all the different colours and coats of paint have been applied, finish off with two to three coats of water-based flooring lacquer (clear varnish). The first coat will need to dry for at least 24 hours; subsequent coats take considerably less time.

Slate & ceramic floor

The marriage of cool grey slate, small vivid blue ceramic tiles and white stones is an evocative combination that picks up on several North African materials, giving them a contemporary twist.

If you have an existing concrete or wooden floor, make sure it is level and fully prepared before tiling. New concrete floors should be screeded to give a flat surface, then prepared with a coat of floor adhesive before applying a layer of plywood as a base on which to work. Wooden floorboards should be similarly covered.

Before buying any materials, work out your floor measurements and design, then calculate the quantities you need. Small ceramic tiles are widely available in sheet form, so are easy to trim to your desired configuration and to mount on plywood for the required depths. The stones can usually be found at garden centres (nurseries), the slate tiles at home decorating stores.

Although it is possible to ensure the slate and mosaic tiles and stones form an even surface to prevent tripping, this project works best in rooms that are not used by children or the elderly.

MATERIALS AND TOOLS

• Plywood, pre-cut to cover the floor surface
• Steel rule • Pencil • Grey slate tiles, measuring 15 x 15cm (6 x 6in) • Small ceramic tiles • Pre-cut plywood squares • Tile adhesive • Narrow-blade paint scraper
• Small white stones • Tile cement

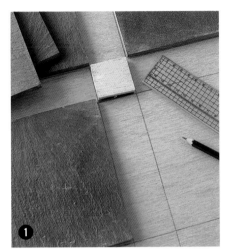

METHOD

First, cover your existing flooring with the sheet of plywood.

❶ Using the steel rule and pencil, mark out your grid on the plywood flooring. As you work, lay the slates and plywood squares onto the grid to make sure you are happy with your design.

❷ With a narrow-blade paint scraper, apply tile adhesive to the areas of the floor where the grey slates are to be positioned. Press each slate firmly into place.

❸ As the slates are thicker than the ceramic tiles, you will need to fix a matching square of plywood under the tiles to bring them up to the same height as the slates. To do this, divide up the sheet of mosaic tiles into squares of four tiles. Dab on four spots of tile adhesive to the back of each square and press firmly onto a corresponding plywood

square. Then glue the combined plywood and ceramic tiles in place on the flooring.

❹ Apply tile cement to the uncovered borders of flooring and slowly pour a quantity of white stones into the cement. Press the stones down gently until as little cement as possible shows through the gaps. Leave the cement to dry for 24 hours before walking on it. For extra protection, seal the stones with a coat of acrylic varnish.

WINDOWS & DOORS

Whatever the cultural context or architectural style, openings in buildings always have a special significance. Windows and doors – the areas of exchange between indoors and out – are important in both a practical and psychological sense, permitting movement and admitting light and air, but more symbolically framing and defining the relationship between interior space and the world outside. They are thresholds, both literally and metaphorically.

In Southern and Eastern societies, windows and doors have often received special decorative attention. Accented with colour and pattern or screened with elaborate latticework, they provide a focus of architectural detail in otherwise simple surroundings. At the same time, especially in cultures where women have traditionally been segregated and largely confined indoors, such embellishment can have an almost poignant significance, with the decorative emphasis drawing attention to the forbidden freedoms of the outside world. Like the enclosed balconies of North Africa or the intricate South American miradors – screened windows projecting onto the

A mustard-coloured banner curtain of heavy cotton edged with a thin border of purplish red catches the breeze in an ornately carved doorway, cooling down the interior.

Right   *Intricately carved panelling in a variety of designs is an enclosing device that sends out an intriguing pattern of shadows on this walkway in the deserted city of Fatehpur Sikri, India.*

Below   *Bright colours are an intrinsic part of the exterior landscape in Haiti. The two tones of russet and aqua on these shutters and door make a striking and cheerful combination.*

street – elaborate decoration can be the means of providing a vantage point where women could see but not be seen.

Inevitably, climatic control has had an impact on the way windows and doors are traditionally treated. In the North, heavy drapery was favoured as a way of keeping out draughts and preventing heat loss in winter. In summer, when fresh air and light were more welcome, these were supplanted by thinner curtains. In the South, the design of vernacular buildings has often kept the interior shaded from strong sunlight, with openings recessed into thick walls and screened so that the power of light is diminished but cooling air can still flow freely.

In the modern, centrally heated and air-conditioned home, there is less need for the tempering effect of window or door treatments, and natural light is increasingly prized in the interior as a means of enhancing space and inspiring a feeling of well-being. And except in the case of the bleakest or busiest outlooks, views provide a valuable connection with the natural world outside. In such a context, exotic window and door treatments are more applicable than ever before. Translucent panels of fabric, slatted screens and blinds at the windows and decorative door surrounds serve to heighten the importance of these essential architectural features.

Above   *Although unadorned, this long, slim, panelled window still creates dramatic impact. Simple downlighters punctuate the wall either side to supplement the discreet amount of light the window allows into the room.*

Right   *Latticed metal lanterns create a rich, warm glow and send mysterious shadows over the floors and walls and around the arched open doorway that frames the open balcony beyond.*

FRAMING THE VIEW

Views through internal spaces and from indoors to the world outside increase the sense of space – a quality that is hugely valued in contemporary design. Views are the way we redress the claustrophobia of modern urban living; they give us a sense of perspective and psychological breathing space. But the whole concept of a 'view' can be fundamentally different in other cultures, and this in turn has an effect on the way doors and windows are treated.

In many areas of the world, views are often inward-looking, through interconnecting suites of rooms or to internal courtyards; views onto busy streets and public areas are usually much more restricted and also heavily screened. This is particularly so in some Islamic cultures where women are traditionally segregated. In Japan, by contrast, the 'view' is imbued with a Zen sensibility. Opaque door and window screens create a contemplative aesthetic for indoor spaces, with small-scale tantalizing glimpses of the natural world standing in for more expansive panoramas. Such minimalism of effect, which pervades traditional Japanese design, is intended to heighten asethetic appreciation by limiting what is on display. The opposite approach is evident in the design of some contemporary houses in Australia. Here, modern architects, drawing inspiration from the elemental qualities of the surrounding landscape, increasingly omit door and window coverings altogether in a natural and emotional response to climate and location. With such a degree of openness, the house is reduced to a simple covering shelter, similar in spirit to traditional Southeast Asian village dwellings, and the notion of a 'view' becomes next to redundant as indoors and outdoors merge.

Architectural detail has a tendency to be minimal in many simple, vernacular houses, which places the onus on decoration as a way of emphasizing and articulating interior space. At its most basic, such decoration can take the form of outlining or framing features such as doors, windows and alcoves – areas where the plane of the wall is naturally interrupted. It is not so very different from framing a picture: the effect is to highlight and focus on what is on view. In contemporary design, too, minimal detailing is the order of the day, an approach that leaves windows as unadorned as possible and treats doors as plain articulated panels within the surface of the wall. In the modern exotic fusion, the trick is to keep a fine balance between simplicity and decorative effect. Too much detail and the end result will be a meaningless hodge-podge; if there is too little emphasis, you won't know why you bothered. The solution is to opt for strong, bold statements, using colour as the foundation for the scheme.

There is nothing like a dash of colour to get a point across. Jazzy borders in clashing colours make vivid frames for the views revealed by windows and doors, and add a

Above   *Sometimes window openings form a major part
of an interior. This partly bricked-up opening is balanced
visually with a small set of concrete steps that allows the
window to double as a doorway.*

Left   *Courtyards and patios become comfortable outdoor
rooms when the climate is willing. This shady backyard seems
as enclosed as an indoor living room, thanks to the carefully
placed container plants. Low-level sofas and a sturdy wooden
table are finished with bamboo legs to blur still further the
boundaries between inside and out.*

great sense of theatricality. Painting window or door frames in a strong colour that reverberates with the colour of the main wall provides instant uplift; for extra definition you can go one step further and extend the effect onto the surrounding wall surface. Repetitive patterns, such as spotted, striped or zigzagged contours, have a strong primitive look. For an earthy effect, try outlining a window or door with a filigree of white motifs stencilled or painted freehand over a terracotta ground. The strength of such decoration is perfect in circumstances where the opening in question is not covered – open archways, for example, or windows that need no screening – and it is also successful if frames and architraves are very simple or even non-existent.

Borders of applied materials work in a similar fashion. Beads, mirror mosaic, pebbles, sequins, tiny shards of tile – virtually anything that will bring colour and glitter to the surface – make evocative decorative surrounds when embedded into the plaster or stuck straight onto the wall. Keep the individual elements small in scale so the total effect of the border does not end up being overwhelming.

For a more sculptural look, you can replace standard architraves with sections of carved panelling. This effect often looks best on a grand scale, as a monumental frame for an open archway, for example, and in contexts where the rest of the decoration is more muted and subdued.

Pelmets (valances) are another way of giving emphasis to openings. Hung or fixed high above the opening, they increase the sense of height and give visual importance; fixed lower down, they can reduce over-sized windows or doors to a more human scale. Standard pelmets generally consist of box-like constructions either upholstered in fabric or painted to blend in with the decorative scheme. For more exotic versions, you could use torans, which are shaped fabric friezes originally from India. These richly encrusted and embroidered textiles, designed to be used on ceremonial occasions such as weddings and festivals, can be hung over doors or windows for instant ethnic flavour. Alternatively, you can construct your own shaped pelmet using thin plywood cut out in a fretted design – perhaps a Moorish-style arch – and painted or covered in punched zinc. Such decorative effects, however, need plenty of breathing space to avoid looking too self-consciously ethnic.

Left *Shutters are as important as windows in hot and sunny parts of the world. Here, French windows with integral shutters save on space and light in a Mediterranean bedroom. Painted in ice-cream shades of pistachio and pink, they create the impression that the beach is not so very far away.*

Far left *Bathing next to open doors and beneath a skylight is as close as you can get to nature without risking embarrassment. A large mirror placed alongside the bathtub means the view can be fully appreciated while bathing.*

FILTERING THE LIGHT

Light is another issue that throws cultural differences into relief. In equatorial and tropical regions, light means heat, and interiors are the only refuge from what can be punishing extremes of temperature. To keep houses cool, windows are often covered with some form of latticework or screening, which takes the strength from the sun. In the contemporary Western interior, by contrast, less is always more, and this is especially true when it comes to window treatments. Wherever possible, the modern instinct is to leave windows uncovered to admit as much light as possible, especially if the window has a pleasant aspect. There are times, however, when even the most ardent minimalist, dedicated to transparency, needs a little privacy.

Oddly, the two approaches can share a common meeting ground. Exotic-style blinds and screens work well in many modern interiors where heavy drapery, elaborate swags and tails and the fussier sort of fabric blinds would strike a discordant note. Fabric-based window treatments that diffuse or filter the light without blocking it entirely are also in keeping with the look. In either case, a suggestion of exoticism is enough. You do not need to worry about strict authenticity; given the different contexts of climate and natural light, there would be little point in any case.

The style of window treatment you choose can help balance an exotic look in a contemporary home. Although window treatments are generally made of fabric, in a room that is otherwise filled with rugs and textiles, the modern edge can quite easily be smothered. In such surroundings, it can be more effective to opt for a harder look at the window, using screens, blinds or shutters, to act as a counterpoint to layers of soft furnishing. On the other hand, semi-transparent drapery, simply suspended at the window, has a floaty ethereal look that contrasts well with pure modern lines and softens some of the severity.

Above   *An interesting variation on a traditional airbrick, this Moorish-style opening doubles as a discreet window and patterned light filter.*

Left   *Embossed, printed and dyed muslins never fail to disguise an ugly window. They also screen out some of the light, so that it does not flood a room, and provide a degree of privacy.*

Far left   *These contemporary, keyhole-shaped stained glass windows are worlds away from traditional Victorian windows and closer in feel to graphic panels of light.*

FABRIC TREATMENTS

When it comes to choosing fabric, you really are spoiled for choice. There is a huge range of suitable materials, both natural and synthetic, but natural, hand-woven and hand-dyed fabrics are probably the best. Sources range from department stores to street markets, with the more interesting and unusual examples often found in specialist shops. You do not have to restrict yourself to what is specifically marketed as furnishing fabric – dress materials can be just as effective decorating a window as they are for making clothes.

Linen, a hard-wearing natural fabric with an ancient pedigree, has a pleasing neutrality, its weave interestingly backlit when draped unlined against a window. In plain white or off-white, or in the natural shades of tomato red, green, dark brown or mulberry, the basic integrity of the material needs little embellishment. Its weight makes it particularly suited to simple treatments where it hangs in soft, loose folds.

Less robust, and much less expensive, are coarse Indian cottons, available in a range of colours from ivory to midnight blue. Many ready-made curtains, which hang from fabric ties, are made of such material. Other cotton fabrics include robust canvas for making crisp, banner-like hangings, plain calico (heavy muslin) and cotton duck.

For a note of sheer indulgence, silk makes sumptuous window treatments. Rough tussore, dyed naturally, has a textural

quality and an appealingly irregular slubbed weave. Silk taffeta, especially the iridescent variety, shot through with glints of contrasting colour, is supremely luxurious.

Finer still are diaphanous drifts of voile, sheer muslin or chiffon, billowing out in filmy clouds with each breath of air. Butter muslin is the lightest of all cotton fabrics and very inexpensive, while chiffon has a harem-style glamour of its own.

For a more overtly homespun take, coarse hessian (burlap) and jute fabrics work well in interiors where the emphasis is on elemental contrasts of texture and material quality. Hessian now comes in a range of colours as well as the standard biscuit brown. To enhance the basic look you can leave edges raw and unfinished and tease them out to make deep fringes.

Above right   *In summer, layers of light muslin are all that is needed to maintain privacy and allow the light to filter through. Heavier curtains can simply be added in winter.*

Above left   *Generous hessian (burlap) curtains hung either side of an entranceway enclose a room and soften the hard edges of the stairs and walls.*

Far left   *In this mix of the classic and the contemporary, a sinuous chaise longue and heavy brocade curtains, together with a glass-topped table, prove that luxurious exoticism is always easy on the eye.*

well. Cream wool or crewelwork on a cream ground can be effective in more neutral schemes, while ikat, bandini, mud-resist and block-printed geometrics such as kente cloth are bold and graphic. Sari fabric, woven through with glittering metallic thread, is the cheat's chic – instant exoticism simply draped or gathered in luscious folds.

Dyeing fabrics extends the decorative possibilities further. Try contrasting swathes of clashing colours: panels of crimson and purple, blue and green, saffron and scarlet overhung so that the light blends the colours together. Tie-dye can also suggest the right mood if you restrict yourself to one or two strong colours and resist creating pyschedelic sunbursts. Another simple technique is to allow dye to soak halfway up a length of lightweight absorbent fabric and then dip the other end in a strong contrasting or toning shade to let the colours bleed into one another. For a finishing touch, add a scattering of beads or sequins sewn across the fabric or as a delicate sparkling border banding each leading edge and hem.

Simple headings are better than formal or tailored effects. At the most basic, fabric can be clipped to fine rods or poles with café clips or tied on with fabric tapes or ribbons. Ruched or cased headings often work well with light, transparent material such as muslin or chiffon. Fine lengths of bamboo can be used for curtain poles if the fabric is light; alternatively choose wrought-iron metal rods for a strong graphic contrast.

Above   A portico acts as decoration inside and out of this roughly panelled room, while the tartan-printed muslin is a contemporary twist on the more ethnic varieties of the fabric usually seen in India. Together they make the walls and windows the main feature of an otherwise simple room.

Right   An intricately embroidered pelmet (valance) cut into a gently domed shape masks an uninteresting window and makes a cosy enclosed space when softened with muslin drapes.

Pattern is abstract rather than representational, and traditional motifs can introduce an unwelcome historical feel. This rules out the bedsit (dorm-room) solution of curtains fashioned from a pair of Indian bedspreads, as well as any obviously ethnic-inspired patterning like paisley. Animal prints such as zebra- and leopard-skin, however, are sufficiently tongue-in-cheek to pass muster and any tone-on-tone pattern, whether embroidered or dyed, always works

Above   Simple, wooden Venetian blinds lend themselves to a variety of exotic styles, from Japanese minimalism to contemporary ethnic. Their presence never dominates a room as they allow the architecture to speak for itself.

Right   The trusty bamboo blind, with its obvious exotic appeal, never goes out of fashion since it is the ultimate inexpensive, practical and aesthetic window covering.

Far right   Adjustable louvred shutters are perfect in warmer climates where they block out enough light at night to act as exterior curtains. Fabric drapes soften the overall look and provide additional warmth.

BLINDS AND SCREENS

Blinds are a versatile and adaptable form of window covering that combine clean modern lines with echoes of hot country living.

Plain roller blinds made of coarse textural fabric such as hessian (burlap), as opposed to pristine white holland, lend a positively ethnic character to a window. Fine cane blinds are inexpensive and widely available in a range of colours as well as the standard natural shade. Venetian blinds, the hard-edged contemporary choice, acquire a softer look when they are made out of wood: finishes range from blond to rich teak or mahogany. Half-open, so that bands of light slant across the room, they generate an instantly moody atmosphere.

Fixed screens, filigree carved panels and louvred shutters also suit the style: in many areas of the world, windows are left unglazed, with such coverings performing the dual function of basic security and light control. Hinged or folding screens covered in translucent rice paper have a look of Eastern serenity. Delicate carved panels or wrought-iron grilles fixed to window frames filter the light in the manner of lace curtains, creating fine patterns of light and shade. Louvres, especially when they are painted in soft dusty colours or bleached-out pastels, have a Caribbean feel about them. Alternatively, for a vivid contemporary culture clash, hang up plastic bead curtains; the gaudy rainbow colours encapsulate a gaiety that works well with the look.

DECORATIVE DOORS

Colour, as ever, is the direct route to creating an exotic look. Sensational shades of fuschia, ultramarine, canary yellow or turquoise can transform standard doors into vibrant entranceways. Panelled doors will lose their sobriety with mouldings and panels picked out in contrasting singing shades, while modern flush doors will gain a revitalizing lease of life if decorated in burnished metallic tones of gold or silver. Glossy ebony black is another evocative finish, providing great graphic contrast for earth-toned decoration.

Texture also has a role to play. In a contemporary interior, the contrast between pristine surfaces and rugged, robust wooden doors can be extremely effective, while in vernacular buildings from India to North Africa, many entrance doors are elaborately carved, inlaid with ebony or mother-of-pearl or painted with intricate patterns to emphasize their symbolic and practical importance.

You can easily distress existing doors by stripping off old finishes and bleaching with liming wax, gesso or white paint rubbed well into the grain to suggest a weatherbeaten and sundrenched look. Alternatively, hunt around salvage yards for old planked doors with a rough-and-ready finish. Accentuate the sense of solidity by adding on metal studs in simple geometric patterns – round-headed brass upholstery tacks can be very effective – or encrusting with sequins, gilt stars or mirror mosaic.

As it is important to encourage the cooling flow of air through the rooms in hot climates, solid interior doors are less common than louvred or pierced screens. One simple way of suggesting a hot country aesthetic is to remove internal doors and adopt one of the window treatments mentioned earlier to screen the opening. Double doorways can be curtained, either with floaty panels of lightweight translucent fabric or more richly patterned and decorative hangings caught back and tied to the frame. Bead curtains hung in open doorways add a veil of colour and make an evocative clicking and swishing as you pass to and fro. Plastic strip door curtains are a bargain-basement alternative. The banner-like Japanese *noren*, which hangs halfway down the door frame, is a more literal borrowing.

To take the effect a step further, you can replace solid interior doors with hinged pairs of latticed, louvred or metal fretwork panels. Painted in light pastel colours, shuttered doors have a colonial look, while elaborate grilled gates are more suggestive of a Moorish style. For an elegantly minimal look, you can replace standard doors with sliding Japanese-style panels, or *fusuma*, covered in translucent rice paper or thin sheets of frosted Perspex (Plexiglas).

Wrought-ironwork, curved and shaped into organic shapes, swirls and twirls, is a feature of chic urban doorways in Paris or Milan but takes its cue from North Africa.

Above   *Beaded curtains are delicate dividers, more often used for decorative purposes than as fluid doors. This one is made from plastic beads, but feathers, shells, plastic streamers and metal links are also suitable materials.*

Dream-catcher bead curtain

Dividing space with a flowing, transparent curtain is an eye-catching way of physically separating two areas of the home, at the same time maximizing natural light and allowing the easy flow of people in and out of the room. Enjoying the sensation of parting a curtain to access another space heightens the feeling of enclosure and provides a vivid counterpoint to neutral colours on the walls and floors. This curtain is a decorative element in its own right, rather than a purely functional door, combining the essence of Native American aesthetics with a sense of colour from Central America.

If you suspect that these beads and feathers might be just a little too bright for your decorating scheme, consider cork, pebbles, dried seed heads and leaves for a natural backdrop, or try colourful glass beads combined with clear Perspex (Plexiglas) for a glass effect, or coloured handmade paper – in fact, anything that is delicate and has an interesting texture. For the string, use thick jute, heavy cord, yacht rope or even strong wire for lashing around specific objects. The header can be made of wood, cut neatly to fit the doorway, or from a piece of gnarled driftwood, Perspex (Plexiglas), wooden dowelling or metal tubing.

MATERIALS AND TOOLS

• One length of 5 x 2.5cm (2 x 1in) soft-wood, cut to fit the width of your opening
• Screw eyes to be fixed at 10cm (4in) intervals • Coloured cord in red, yellow and

orange, 8m (9yds) of each colour • Sewing thread in coordinating colours • Brightly dyed feathers • Sticky tape • Wooden beads in purple and pink (20 of each) • Plastic beads in orange, yellow and blue (100 of each) • Neon-coloured, plastic bendy drinking straws • Curtain weights or heavy beads

METHOD

First, screw a section of 5 x 2.5cm (2 x 1in) softwood in your doorway or opening to use as a header for the curtain. Divide the length of wood into equal intervals, appropriate to the space being screened, and screw in the screw eyes. For this doorway, which measured 2m (6½ft) deep by 75cm (2½ft) wide, intervals of 10cm (4in) were used.

❶ Cut lengths of coloured cord to the required depth of your doorway or opening, allowing an extra 7.5cm (3in) for attaching to the header. Tie the feathers to the cord at intervals using sewing thread.

❷ Place sticky tape at the end of the cord to form a 'needle' for threading on the drinking straws, beads and so on at random intervals, interspersing them between the more solid 'stoppers' of feathers to create a pleasing informal arrangement. At the end of each run, knot the thread at the bottom, making sure that different objects are used to finish off each run of the curtain. To stop the cords billowing in the breeze, fix curtain weights or beads to the end of each cord.

Decorative shutters

Shutters are not only for hot climates where they keep out the sun and seal in the cool air. Painted, decorated and used half-height, they will cheer up an urban apartment or a rural room, creating a sense of the exotic. These shutters are made from two layers of MDF (particleboard), glued and nailed together, then decorated in colours drawn from the Far East. An air of faded splendour is introduced with gold burnishing cream, which is perfect for edging and detailing or as a decorative accent. MDF can be pre-cut to your requirements, while ready-made decorative edging is available in metre (yard) lengths. The shutters shown here are for decoration only. If you want your shutters to close, you will need to decorate both sides.

MATERIALS AND TOOLS

For one shutter, you will need:
• One base panel in 12mm (½in) deep MDF (particleboard), measuring half the length and width of the window area to be covered • Decorative strip for the top outside edge of the shutter, approximately 6mm (¼in) deep, measuring the width of the base panel • Two vertical insert panels in 6mm (¼in) deep MDF, cut to fit • Two horizontal insert panels in 6mm (¼in) deep MDF, cut to fit • Decorative edge trims, approximately 6mm (¼in) deep, to fit around the inside edge of the horizontal and vertical panels • Tenon (fine-toothed) saw • Pencil • Ruler • Set square • Poster paint in brown, pink and sand • Soft cloth • Gold burnishing cream • Wood adhesive • Hammer • Panel pins (tacks) • Sandpaper • 4 x face-fixing butterfly hinges • Screws • Tape measure • 10cm (4in) paintbrush • 12mm (½in) paintbrush • Cotton buds • Acrylic matt varnish • Primer • Paintbrushes • White matt base paint

METHOD

Each shutter is made from a base panel of MDF measuring half the width of the window area you wish to cover. The top of the shutter is edged with a decorative strip, and the inside with plain horizontal and vertical panels and decorative edge trims.

1 Cut the panels and decorative edging to fit using a tenon saw. On the base panel, using a pencil and ruler, mark the positions of the decorative strip that will run along the top of the shutter, the horizontal and vertical panels, and the decorative edge trims.

Using wood adhesive, glue the decorative strip a few millimetres in on the top front edge of the base panel. Hammer in a few panel pins along the back edge to give extra support. Leave to dry before gluing on the two horizontal and vertical strips. Allow a few millimetres extra on the length of these additional strips so you can sand them back to fit flush. Use a set square to ensure

the pieces are correctly in place. Finally, fix the edge trims within the framework you have created, using wood adhesive and nails to secure firmly. Paint on a coat of primer and allow to dry.

2 Apply one coat of white base paint over the whole shutter. Mix a little of the pink and sand paints and water into the brown paint to create a shade of faded red. Use a 10cm (4in) brush to lightly apply one coat all over the shutter except for the decorative strip and edge trims. As soon as you have brushed on the paint, wipe it down with a soft, damp cloth to give a streaky effect, but leave a narrow band of solid colour on the base panel adjacent to the edge trims.

3 Apply gold burnishing cream to the edge trims with a 12mm (½in) paintbrush; use cotton buds for more awkward areas, such as around the edge trims. Finish off with a coat or two of acrylic matt varnish over the

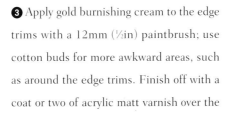

complete shutter to protect the surface. Repeat all the above steps on the second panel to make a pair of shutters. Screw two butterfly hinges onto each shutter and fix securely to the wall.

FURNITURE & FURNISHINGS

FURNITURE & FURNISHINGS

Furniture design enshrines attitudes to living. No one is quite sure why the world seems to divide broadly into cultures where sitting on the floor has always been the norm or where sitting on chairs is the preferred option. One might argue that floor-level living is more informal, but there is nothing informal about traditional Japanese culture with its precise rituals and courtesies. Neither can chair cultures be assumed to be more prosperous and advanced. Sitting off the ground, if only on benches or stools, has long been favoured in the West, even in the poorest sectors of society and in the darkest of ages. Climate may have some part to play, but it is far from a deciding factor. What is clear is that over the last few decades these two strands of development have increasingly converged, resulting in a fusion of modern and exotic styles.

Cross-influences have been in operation for some time, although in many cases cultural exchange has resulted in strange hybrids. The British introduced various types of European furniture to India where, apart from beds, few such items had existed before. Indian furniture still displays a certain lack of concern with what might be called classical proportional relationships, but this is not surprising, given that, for thousands of years, the culture managed perfectly well without very much furniture at all and therefore had no need to learn the design language. The late nineteenth century saw a European enthusiasm for all things Japanese; no one in the West seemed particularly bothered about the contradiction in terms represented by Japanese-style tables, chairs and whatnots – pieces that for all their lacquered and bamboo finishes would have looked as alien in the traditional Japanese house as a crinoline or frock coat.

In the twentieth century, the increasing informality of lifestyle, the trend for open-plan arrangement and the predominating long, low horizontal lines of many modern interiors have, perhaps somewhat unwittingly, come much closer to the aesthetic of floor-sitting cultures. The Japanese house was, and still is, a powerful point of reference for many modern architects and designers, but the contemporary taste for getting back to basics by concentrating on elemental, simple forms has also had a part to play. Today, within this sympathetic framework, exotic influences expressed in the design of furniture and furnishings look much more at home.

Left   A collection of silk cushions in various vibrant hues provides sharp punctuation for this ornate carved backdrop.

Right   In a true fusion of Eastern, Western and rustic influences, this living room is at once cosy and informal, modern and understated.

ARRANGEMENT

Furniture arrangement implies the optimum positioning of tables and chairs, sofas and stools, chests and beds, juggled within a finite space until the perfect combination is achieved. It implies having plenty of furniture to arrange – and suggests that achieving a successful result demands more or less the same type of skills as those required to complete a moderately difficult jigsaw puzzle.

In contemporary exotic decorating, furniture is simpler and thinner on the ground. Arrangement becomes less about fitting things together and more about achieving a harmonious balance, where the room and whatever it contains read as a unified whole. It is outward-looking as well, connecting with exterior spaces beyond the immediate boundaries of four walls.

Minimalism has a lot to do with it. One of the most significant Eastern influences of recent times has been the emergence of near-empty, Zen-inspired rooms as the height of interior fashion. Less has always been more for modern architects and designers, and for those at the cutting edge, almost nothing is increasingly everything. While only a few people actively choose to live in such pure surroundings, the impact of minimalism as a style has been to encourage a lighter, less cluttered look in the mainstream of contemporary taste. The Victorians were apparently unable to manage without myriad occasional tables, each laden with its own cargo of lace doilies and china knick-knacks, but we are smothered by the very idea of such density. The inevitable outcome is that contemporary rooms cannot help but be closer in spirit to many global vernacular styles.

Density, or lack of it, has an impact on arrangement. What remains when a space has been largely emptied out has a certain

Left   An inspiring mix of wood tones on walls, ceiling and furniture produces a cool, cohesive scheme in an Indonesian interior.

Below   Floor cushions and low-level furniture are the key to achieving the exotic look in this period room.

The unpainted rafters and neutral tones in this loft space create a peaceful haven. A bathtub is sunk into a concrete plinth next to the window, while a beech-framed bed is simply dressed with white cotton bed linen.

The hierarchical arrangement of separate rooms, where each one is devoted to a specific purpose, is often missing in vernacular houses, with the consequence that furniture and furnishings tend not to be designed for specific locations and so lend themselves to being transported from area to area and used as and when the need arises.

unavoidable presence that makes its own demands. In theory, if a room contains only a few pieces of furniture, there are dozens of ways they can be arranged, but in practice only a few of these will look and feel natural. In this context, symmetry can be an important means of achieving a sense of poise and calm. Aligning furniture with main axes through spaces, pairing seats, cushions and tables and avoiding skewed or casual layouts promotes a tranquil atmosphere.

Paying attention to the relationship with existing architectural features, such as fireplaces, doors and windows, so that furniture is positioned in sympathy with its surroundings is also critical. In northern climates, opportunities to extend living areas into outdoor spaces, such as courtyards, terraces and gardens, are necessarily more limited than in areas where the weather is more benign, but a more integrated approach can be effected by using similar materials and furniture indoors and out.

The ancient Chinese discipline of feng shui, which is currently enjoying a faddish success in the West, has many rules concerning spatial arrangement. Many of these amount to little more than common sense. In feng shui the basic aim is simply to promote a feeling of well-being by avoiding what is discordant and irregular – features such as sharp angles, protruding corners, overhanging beams and awkwardly placed furniture that all work to undermine the natural sense of order.

Although symmetry and order can seem at odds with the modern desire for informal living, there does not necessarily have to be a conflict. With a basic underpinning of order, rooms become more serene and contemplative, which, in turn, promotes a laid-back mood and atmosphere. In a similar way, the modern trend for multi-purpose, open-plan spaces, where activities flow from one area to another, can provide a good foundation for expressing an exotic influence.

Within such fluid arrangements, some form of spatial division may still be necessary. Simple folding screens or shimmering, veil-like hangings of semi-transparent fabric take the place of more permanent dividers to partition areas or create the suggestion of enclosure in an open-plan space. Screens are not particularly difficult to make and a wide range of materials and finishes, from plain wooden panels to fabric-covered frameworks, can be most effective. For an organic textural quality, choose screens of woven rush or thin lengths of cane; traditional Japanese rice paper screens are spare and elegant; rich lacquerwork, inlaid with intricate designs, adds a dash of exotic flavour.

Japanese rooms are always free of clutter, beautifully proportioned and carefully furnished. Tatami mats are used as flooring and rice paper screens as room dividers, while the floor-to-ceiling windows allow the composite whole to be fully appreciated from all angles.

SEATS AND TABLES

We naturally have a tendency to identify floor-level living as informal, which is one of the reasons we are attracted to cultural styles where such a practice is the norm. Lounging on the floor, or sitting on cushions or low platforms or stools, appeals to the Western sense of the democratic as it brings everyone down to the same level.

Unlike perching on the edge of an upright chair, sitting on the floor is literally down to earth. It is a posture without status or pretension. Of course, there is an element of wilful misconception about the whole issue: certainly, traditional Japanese society was far from free and easy, despite the fact that most everyday activities took place in close proximity to the floor. And when we copy the Near Eastern custom of sitting on carpets, we do not borrow the rest of the peripatetic lifestyle and choose to live in tents. It is merely that, from a Western perspective, the lower the seating level, the higher the apparent degree of relaxation – mental or behavioural relaxation, that is. Unfortunately, years of sitting on chairs mean that for most people in the West, apart from the very young or supple, the floor is not as physically comfortable as it might be. Fortunately, there is a halfway house. Marrying the low-slung lines of contemporary seat furniture with floor cushions, simple stools and benches transforms the floor into more of a hospitable surface for day-to-day living.

Unlike the dominating presence of the three-piece suite – overstuffed sofa with matching easy chairs ranged mindlessly in front of the television set – seating in an exotic interior is a carefully judged ensemble where no single piece steals the limelight. Simple modern furniture, such as long upholstered benches, low rectilinear sofas and basic utilitarian stools, provide the contemporary edge. Improvised seats, consisting of nothing more elaborate than a mattress or a piece of foam covered with fabric, matting or a rug, work just as well as more conspicuous design statements. Tatami mats, half-flooring, half-seating, make low platforms for lounging or a resilient base for cushions. Outdoor furniture, such as slatted teak or iroko benches, create a sense of integration between indoor and outdoor areas. Handmade exotic artefacts, such as carved African stools, provide a signature note.

Left   In this ultra-simple dining room, the narrow refectory table and folding chairs show that simplicity can be just as exotic as excess. The star-shaped spotlights provide all the necessary decoration.

Right   In this dining room, industrial design meets traditional Japanese style, combining oriental panelling and exotic flowers with modern Danish chairs.

Cushions break out of their traditional role as accessories to become essential elements. Large square floor cushions, bean bags, long bolsters and hide-covered pouffes (ottomans) provide support for floor-level sitting and a softer, textural quality to contrast with elemental shapes and materials. Piled in symmetrical arrangements on low divans or matting, the look is the antithesis of the cluttered 'hippy' apartment.

Low tables accompany low seating areas. Simple, chunky shapes in dark wenge wood, zebrano or iroko combine the pure lines of modern design with the raw appeal of natural materials. Plinths of cast concrete or stone, which have been set on low bases, have a strong primitive appeal. Antique Indian day beds double as coffee tables to bring a focus to an arrangement. Indian brass tea tables, which are essentially trays on legs, are another option to consider, while metal tables with mosaic or tiled tops give a Moorish flavour.

For those dedicated to floor-level living, eating areas can share the same aesthetic, making the perfect surroundings for enjoying the fusion flavours of world cuisine. But most of us still feel more comfortable sitting rather higher up when we eat our meals. Simple modern tables and chairs are sufficiently anonymous to be in keeping with the modern exotic look; plain refectory-style tables and benches are even better. Look out for stone- or metal-topped tables, which introduce the element of material quality.

Above   *When the very fabric of a building is simple and discreet, why spoil it with too much furniture? Low, rectilinear sofas and a chunky coffee table provide all the necessary comfort in this contemporary Balinese interior.*

Right   *A clash of cultures in the form of oriental accessories and Thirties-style, modernist architecture and design is a surprisingly winning combination.*

BEDS

Different cultures are no more alike in their sleeping habits than in their sitting habits. In some parts of the world, sleeping requires little more than a mattress, rolled up and stored during the day when not in use; in other cultures, even where people are devoted to floor-sitting, beds are preferred.

Futons are the obvious choice for those keen to maintain the low profile of floor-level living. These Japanese mattresses, stuffed with waddings of wool, cotton or coconut fibres, have excellent ecological and health credentials. They have become increasingly popular in the West as one of the simplest and most economical forms of sofa bed around, and for the ease with which they can be transformed into simple low seats during the day. Futons are traditionally laid directly on the ground; in the West, they are sold more often in conjunction with pallet-like bases in wood or metal. Low divan beds or even standard mattresses placed on the floor have a similar aesthetic. For a more considered look and greater resilience, mattresses could also be placed on top of a springy tatami mat.

Metal bedsteads, less self-effacing in style, also work well with the look. French colonial brass beds, white-painted filigree cast-iron, or modern plain or enamelled iron have sufficient presence to take centre stage. Headboards made of wickerwork or woven straw add a textural dimension; carved or lacquered panels supply decorative interest. Contemporary versions of the four-poster, featuring simple wooden or metal uprights, provide the framework for dressing beds with glorious hangings of coloured silk or printed cotton. The romantic flourish of filmy mosquito netting can be hard to resist, even in northern latitudes where the risk of tropical disease and malaria-carrying mosquitoes is admittedly rather slight.

Left *A traditional Japanese futon bed demonstrates the simplicity of low-level living. The floor covering of tatami mats doubles as the base of the bed when a thick mattress is laid over them at the end of each day.*

Above   *Synonymous with elegance and restraint, day beds provide instant relaxation and make versatile furniture for an outdoor living environment. Topped with a thin quilt and cushions of fine raw silks, this bed is placed enticingly close to a water fountain on a cool, tiled floor.*

Left   *This interpretation of the traditional four-poster could not be more elegant or exotic. Powder blue muslin, with inset panels of cream, is suspended from a thin metal frame and drapes down to the rough-painted platform floor.*

FURNISHING MATERIALS

Bold contrasts of materials are the key: modern and traditional, natural and machine-made, soft and hard, textured and decorated, rough and smooth. Furnishing materials – in the form of seat or cushion covers, throws, bed linen and table settings – provide a wide scope for achieving such evocative juxtapositions.

Previous incarnations of ethnic style relied heavily on textiles to create an enveloping mood of exoticism. The lines of furniture were all but obliterated under swathes of fabric, profusely draped and layered in seemingly artless abandon. By contrast, the use of fabrics in a contemporary exotic interior is much more clear cut. Textiles and their tactile dimension are just as important, but the effect is more carefully judged. Instead of loose coverings, there are the taut lines of upholstery to provide a crisp, sharp edge. Instead of layering, there is a more precise placement and a sense of restraint.

Materials are valued for the way they engage with the senses. Leather smells good, feels wonderful and improves with age. In recent years, it has dramatically shed its rather tacky image and is now used to make svelte coverings for cushions, benches, pouffes and padded stools. Butter-soft suede and matt hide in graphic shades of black, tan and chocolate brown have a cool, contemporary appeal. Shaggy fake fur, nubbly rugs and chenille throws pile on the comfort. White, cream or grey linen makes a classic

partnership with dark or ebonized wood in graphic, neutral versions of the style.

Luxurious materials such as velvet, brocade and silk soften the strong lines of the modern interior and provide jewel-bright accents of colour. Silks from India, Cambodia or China in luminous shades of saffron, fuchsia or moody violet delight the eye; sumptuous silk velvets spell instant glamour; delicate brocades, finely woven Ghanaian kente cloth or ikats make a subtle counterpoint to rugged wood or stone surfaces; embroidered and mirrored Gujarati textiles add glitter and sparkle; dress fabrics, such as sarongs and saris, provide an unbeatable source of pattern and colour.

Above *Cream linen contrasts beautifully with the taupe bed covers, contributing to the overall peaceful atmosphere in this streamlined bedroom of oriental elegance.*

Left *Inviting piles of velvet cushions in deep oranges, pinks and reds evoke a palpable warmth and create a richness and abundance impossible to ignore.*

Above   *Tiled walls in intense colours are decoration enough in a functional kitchen. The addition of a large, star-shaped light shade shows how a single element, used sensitively, can produce a distinct exotic look.*

Right   *Furnishings are kept to a minimum in this spacious bathroom, where the freestanding bath is screened off with simple tab-headed curtains suspended on thin metal poles. A carved chair heightens the exotic flavour.*

FIXTURES AND FITTINGS

Kitchens and bathrooms, two of the hardest working areas of the home, provide another fertile meeting ground for the fusion of modern and exotic. Modern reminds us that such areas must be functional and efficient, with fittings, fixtures and services well integrated and operating smoothly. Exotic reminds us of the elemental pleasures of cooking an appetizing meal or soaking away the stresses of the day in scented water.

Behind-the-scenes planning is critical. Tight, workable layouts that maximize the available space and provide an ergonomic flow of activities are just as essential in generously proportioned areas as in more confined spaces where every square inch matters a great deal. Only when the basic framework is right can you go on to consider more decorative issues.

The contemporary kitchen is typically sleek and fitted, the logic of the layout expressed in neat runs of units and smooth surfaces and finishes. An exotic look need not be less pristine, but the elemental qualities of colour and texture provide a more sensual environment for the enjoyment of food and its preparation. It is not really

A miniature bathroom inset into a wall of painted plaster is a reminder of how distinct rooms can be cleverly incorporated into contained spaces. Discreet and neat, this bathtub also benefits from a view across the main room.

necessary to rip out existing features to convey the mood; simple cosmetic alterations are often very effective.

Colour is a key element. A vibrant splash of colour will revive tired door and cupboard fronts and even boring or bland tiling. Almost any material can be painted over if you use the right type of paint. Tile paint comes in many intense exotic hues and can transform a utilitarian splashback into a more resonant, evocative background. It is also simpler and more straightforward than hacking the tiles off and replacing them.

New cupboard doors can also give a kitchen an economical facelift. Tongue-and-groove fronts, painted ice-cream colours, have Caribbean appeal. Plain flush doors embellished with decorative star or crescent cut-outs, with applied motifs in punched tin, or with patterns created with studs, also have an exotic flavour. Doors featuring open grillework or mesh panels are another option, while free-standing dressers and cabinets have a homely quality that also works well with the look.

Worktops provide the perfect opportunity for introducing a textural dimension to a kitchen. Granite, with its rich flecks of colour, thick planks of dark stained wood, and zinc, which acquires a pleasing patina with use, provide a strong counterpoint to modern lines. Tiled surfaces evoke the vernacular styles of Latin America and North Africa.

A taste for exotic decor tends to go along with an appreciation of the cooking of other countries, and, in many cases, the expansion of culinary horizons precedes the widening of visual reference. In the kitchen, utensils that accompany such diverse styles of cooking, from woks to couscousiers, from bamboo steam baskets to tagines, are entirely at home and in frequent use. Open shelves, filled with the gaudy packaging of unusual ingredients, spell out the global theme. Solid, chunky shelving, which looks as if it almost forms part of the wall, has a sculptural quality about it that is totally in keeping with the look. For decorative interest, you can edge shelving with lengths of tin, scalloped or zigzagged, mosaic tiles, gilt stars or beads.

As with kitchens, bathrooms forgo none of the contemporary conveniences, that is, indoor plumbing, reliable hot water and efficient drainage. But bathroom design is also influenced by the variety of approaches to bathing around the world, attitudes that tend to be more firmly rooted in the elemental pleasures of washing than the Western preoccupation with hygiene and sanitation. Communal bathing, from the family soak of Japan to the steam baths and plunge pools of the Near East, introduces a social side to what we frequently regard in the West as a purely private matter. In many cultures, but most notably in Japan, a distinction is also made between cleaning the body and the more sensual benefits of a hot soak: the body is soaped and rinsed before stepping into the tub, or showered before entering the steam room. The Japanese are appalled by the notion of washing and soaking in the same scummy water.

Left *You could not fail to relax in a shower that commanded such a good view of the outdoors through gothic arches. The walls are concrete, with insets of brick, while the floor is tiled.*

Right *This deep, stone bathtub appears to emerge organically from the wall, as if it formed part of the structure of the building.*

Devotees of such approaches to bathing can increasingly turn their preferences into practice. Japanese-style hot tubs, made of cedar, have begun to make an appearance in contemporary minimalist homes. Enthusiasts should be aware, however, that such tubs require daily soaking to remain watertight, otherwise the wood shrinks and leaks develop. Sunken tubs also have an exotic appeal. Those with large enough bathrooms might simply emulate the Japanese example by including a shower for washing as well as a tub for soaking. Rather than opt for a ready-made shower stall in the bathroom, you can partition space to construct a special shower area with a draining floor. The exotic mood often depends on a certain simplicity and directness of experience.

An exotic flavour is heightened by the use of materials. Mosaic and tiles cladding entire surfaces, not as skimpy margins, have a whole-hearted look about them; natural stone and wood make pleasing surfaces to touch and have a rugged, natural aesthetic. Wherever possible, strive for a uniformity of effect, where walls, floors and surfaces are made of the same material.

Keep the rest of the furnishings to a minimum. Simple benches replace bathroom chairs; wall-hung cabinets in basic, rustic-style painted wood conceal bathroom clutter. Old armoires, antique carved chests or plain wickerwork hampers and baskets provide attractive and useful places to keep linen and bathroom accessories.

STORAGE

The modern exotic fusion requires plenty of breathing space, which means that storage needs to be very carefully considered. To maintain the contemplative mood of the style, possessions should be well organized behind the scenes, and certainly not all out on view. The seamless order of the traditional Japanese interior is an important point of reference. Even if you lack the absolute discipline of the minimalist, it is well worth spending some time reviewing what you

own and getting rid of what is redundant, outdated or otherwise superfluous to requirements to lighten the load all round.

Contemporary storage solutions provide an infrastructure to keep possessions under control. The most thorough-going approaches may involve radical reorganization, looking at the way you live and making different use of the available space. Think about creating specific storage zones to subtract clutter from main living areas – these can be 'between spaces' under stairs or on landings, converted spaces in attics or basements, or borrowed spaces, special storage rooms for clothes, linen or books made by partitioning off part of a larger existing room.

In main living areas, storage should be near-invisible. This is particularly important in the bedroom, where an exotic mood can be severely undermined by the presence of everyday clutter. Banish your wardrobe behind sliding floor-to-ceiling panels or the self-effacing doors of neatly integrated closets and cupboards. Fit alcoves with shelves for folding clothes and screen them with a fabric or cane blind. Categorize belongings such as CDs, videos and stationery into systematic boxes made of metal, cardboard or plastic to present a unified front; smaller items can be housed in bright raffia baskets or tin canisters.

Free-standing storage, which makes a focal point in its own right, is also compatible with the style, provided there is some type of exotic element to the design. In fact,

what most cultures have in common, whether they sit on the floor and sleep on mattresses or sit on chairs and sleep in beds, is storage furniture. Chests, cabinets and trunks are the common containers for personal and household belongings the world over. At the most basic, such catch-alls can be no more elaborate than tin trunks or lidded baskets, but many pieces represent the height of craftsmanship and artistry. Often made as part of a bride's dowry or to commemorate the birth of a child,

Left   *In a delightfully simple but purely functional kitchen, a collection of oriental pots provides visual interest alongside the everyday food containers and appliances. The substantial open shelves provide easy access.*

Far left   *A simple stone sink surround incorporates one chunky shelf for towels and toiletries. Wicker baskets, with their exotic overtones, conceal unsightly bathroom paraphernalia.*

beautifully carved, lacquered or inlaid chests and cupboards are as visually stunning as they are practical in design. Fine antiques or handmade examples, such as embossed leather chests from North Africa, Manchurian lacquerwork cabinets, and Javanese carved cupboards, can be rather expensive but they do provide a rich and characterful centrepiece.

More affordably, there are many designs of storage furniture available on the market that have distinctly exotic overtones.

Wardrobes, chests and sideboards in reclaimed teak with bamboo-latticed fronts, colourwashed planked cupboards with fretwork cut-outs, retro burnished metal medicine cabinets and meat safes work well within the context of the aesthetic and provide practical homes for a wide range of belongings. Alternatively, you can customize simple containers such as boxes and trunks by covering them with exotic fabric or paper.

Shelving is the most versatile form of open storage, providing a readily accessible means of organizing and housing practically everything, from books, video tapes and CDs to kitchen china and clothing. Avoid the reticence of many contemporary metal or glass systems, and instead use shelving to express a more substantial quality that enables it to become part of the architecture of the room. Alcove shelves are thick and chunky and widely spaced, while low, horizontal plinths of stone or wood provide a storage platform running around the perimeter of the room.

Tiled worktop

Tiled kitchen worktops are usually plain-coloured, neutral surfaces, but the chalky textured treatment applied to these terracotta tiles produces a faded elegance that is Moorish in its references. The tiles have been decorated using handmade stencils, allowing a greater flexibility of design. You can allow the colours to merge with an existing scheme, or create a colour statement that is a feature in its own right.

Each tile is treated with robust varnish to protect the decoration, while trivets and mats will afford even greater protection from objects hot from the oven. The same decorative technique can be employed elsewhere in the home, especially in bathrooms. Floor tiles can be similarly decorated, although you will need to apply extra coats of heavy-duty varnish to prevent scuffing.

MATERIALS AND TOOLS

• Terracotta tiles, measuring 15 x 15cm (6 x 6in) • Pencil • Stencil card • Scissors • Water-based wood paint or non-vinyl water-based paint in creamy-white (for the background) and a range of soft, muted shades • Paintbrush • Soft cloth • Flat stippling brush • 12mm (½in) wide, low-tack masking tape • Oil-based matt varnish • Tile cement and grout

METHOD

Before applying any paint, decide how you wish to decorate each tile. Mark the designs freehand in pencil onto each tile before

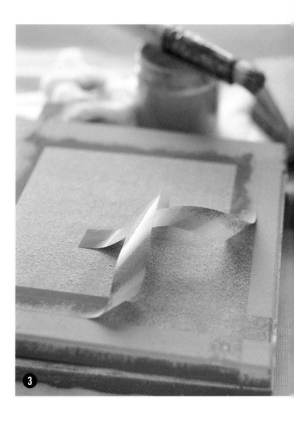

making your stencils. Cut out pieces of stencil card, or non-porous card such as postcards, into squares or rectangles by folding a piece of card in half and cutting out three sides to obtain a geometric template. The motifs can be any shape you like, as long as they are not too intricate.

❶ For the background colour, apply the creamy-white wood paint to each tile with a paintbrush, and immediately wipe some off with a soft cloth to create a wash effect. This will allow the orange tones of the terracotta to show through. (Instead of wood paint, you can use non-vinyl, water-based matt paint.) Leave to dry.

❷ Apply low-tack masking tape to the areas you do not want to be coloured; using 12mm (½in) masking tape allows you to create a greater variety of designs than wider tapes. Then apply the paint through the stencils with a flat stippling brush. Use very small amounts of paint on the brush and hold it at a 90-degree angle. Allow to dry, then apply the next colour.

❸ Remove the masking tape as soon as the paint has dried to prevent any background paint flaking off. Apply two to three coats of varnish to protect the paint. Before cementing and grouting the tiles in place, arrange them loosely on the surface to be covered so that you can be sure of the end result.

Rustic screen

Screening unpleasant views and cluttered corners, or creating a separate area within a room, is best achieved with a free-standing screen. Inspired by the Japanese tradition of screening, this variation is made by weaving green sticks through a simple framework of dowelling attached to chunky, rustic timber. Green sticks are available from specialist florists and flower markets. If you buy them 'fresh', be sure to hang them vertically for a few weeks first to dry them out. Their bright green colour will fade to a softer tone. Cut the sticks so they fit snugly within the frame. As the fibres will dry out and shrink, more sticks will need to be added later. A similar effect can be achieved using ready-made sections of bamboo or cane screening, available from garden centres (nurseries).

MATERIALS AND TOOLS

• 6 wooden posts for the vertical supports, measuring 5 x 5cm (2 x 2in) square by about 150cm (5ft) long • 6 wooden posts for the horizontal struts, measuring 5 x 5cm (2 x 2in) square by about 45cm (18in) long • 15 lengths of dowelling, each 150cm (5ft) long and 6mm (¼in) in diameter • 12 bundles of green sticks, or cane screening, cut to fit • ½ metre (½ yard) hessian (burlap) • Wood stain • Soft cloth • Mitre block • Tenon (fine-toothed) saw • Electric drill • Countersinker • Wood glue • Set square • Screwdriver • 24 crosshead screws, 7.5cm (3in) long • Tape measure and pencil • Craft knife • 48 carpet tacks • Hammer

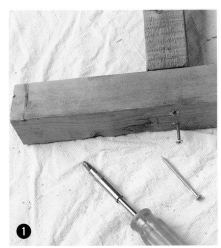

METHOD

First, trim the ends of the horizontal posts with a mitre block and saw to make sure they are completely flat and square. Stain the dowels using a soft cloth. Leave to dry.

❶ Drill two holes in the outside edge of each post, top and bottom, about 15cm (6in) in from the bottom, 7.5cm (3in) in from the top and 12mm (½in) in from each side. Use a countersinker to contour the holes. Apply glue to one end of a cross rail and position it against the first post, aligning the centre of the rail with the holes already drilled in the post. Check that it is at a right angle using the set square, then screw the two pieces of wood together with two 6.5cm (2½in) crosshead screws. Repeat the process on the other side, top and bottom, to form a panel. Make up three panels in this way.

Once you have a complete panel, measure to the centre of each cross rail and make a pencil mark. Measure in about 5cm (2in) on both sides from the vertical posts and mark on the cross rail. Measure the centre points between these marks. Drill five 12mm (½in) holes over each of the five marks, on the top and bottom cross rail.

❷ Cut five pieces of dowelling to the internal distance between the cross rails, plus 2cm (¾in) extra for fitting them into the holes. Slot the dowels into the bottom section first, then ease them into the top holes (this thickness of dowelling is quite flexible). When the dowels are in position, weave the sticks through them by hand, making sure you pack them in as tightly as possible. Repeat for the other two panels.

❸ When each panel is complete, make the hinges using thick hessian (burlap). Cut the fabric into four 15cm (6in) squares, then fold over each side of the square by 12mm (½in) to make 13cm (5in) squares (this means that no hemming is necessary).

Hammer in 12 tacks per hinge, making sure that the folded-over fabric is properly secured. There should be two hinges to each intersecting panel, fixed about 15cm (6in) in from the top and bottom of the screen.

Chunky coffee table

Taking its inspiration from the low-level-living aesthetic found all over the Far East, this understated coffee table fits perfectly into a modern, ethnic-style living room. Clean-lined and looking every bit as sophisticated as a luxurious piece of wenge wood, it is made from a combination of solid beech legs and beech-veneered MDF (particleboard), both stained a dark oak colour to complement a pale colour scheme. The marriage of sleekly contoured wood with the MDF is a happy fake: once the materials are combined and stained, the juxtaposition of real and *faux* is not apparent.

Using veneered MDF, cut to fit from a timber yard (lumberyard), instead of solid wood for the tabletop helped to keep costs down, but because it comes in standard depths, it was necessary to fix two sections together to achieve the desired dimensions.

MATERIALS AND TOOLS

• 2 squares of beech-veneered MDF (particleboard), measuring 60 x 60 x 1.8cm (24 x 24 x ¾in) • 4 sections of solid beech, measuring 7 x 7 x 25cm (2¾ x 2¾ x 10in) • 8 x 7.5cm (3in) crosshead screws • 13 x 3cm (1¼in) crosshead screws • Tape measure • Pencil • Screwdriver • Electric drill and bits • Countersinker • Wood glue • Sandpaper and sanding block • 4 strips of beech veneer, measuring 61 x 5cm (24½ x 2in) • Craft knife • Contact adhesive • Wood stain or dye • Acrylic satin-finish varnish • 10cm (4in) varnish brush • Soft cloth

METHOD

❶ To make the holes for joining together the two pieces of wood for the tabletop, first place one square of MDF on a flat work surface. With a tape measure and pencil, find the central point of the square. Drill a hole and use a countersinker to contour the opening. From each corner, measure 11.5cm (4½in) along each side and 2.5cm (1in) in from the edge, marking all eight points with a pencil. Drill and countersink the holes. Drill and countersink a hole in the middle of each side, 2.5cm (1in) in from the edge.

To make the screw holes for the legs, turn over the square and drill and countersink two holes at each corner, with the first hole measuring 4cm (1½in) from the corner and 2cm (¾in) in from the edge, and the second hole 6cm (2¼in) in from the corner and 2cm (¾in) in from the edge. (You should end up with 13 holes for joining the two squares of wood together and eight for attaching the table legs.)

❷ To attach the legs, drill two holes in the top of each leg to correspond with those on the MDF. Apply wood glue generously (wipe off any excess later with a damp cloth) to the tops and position the drilled square on top of the legs. Screw the legs to the MDF with 7.5cm (3in) countersink screws.

Place the top square of MDF upside down on the work surface and apply wood glue. Carefully lay the other square with the legs attached on top so that the two squares

line up. Screw the 3cm (1¼in) screws into both squares through the existing holes. Once the glue has dried, sand the edges.

To give the table a uniform finish, glue strips of beech veneer to the sides of the table. With a craft knife, cut four pieces of veneer to fit, allowing an extra 6mm (¼in) all round for sanding. Then apply contact adhesive to one side of the tabletop and to one piece of veneer at a time. You will need to let the adhesive dry a little, according to the manufacturer's instructions, before pressing on the veneer. Repeat this procedure for the three remaining sides.

❸ Once the adhesive has dried, sand the joins, holding the sanding block at a 45-degree angle, so that the veneer strips are flush with the rest of the table. Next, apply a coat of dark oak stain with a soft cloth. Finish off with two to three coats of acrylic satin-finish varnish. Allow each coat to dry thoroughly before applying the next.

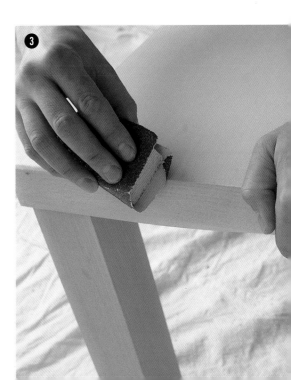

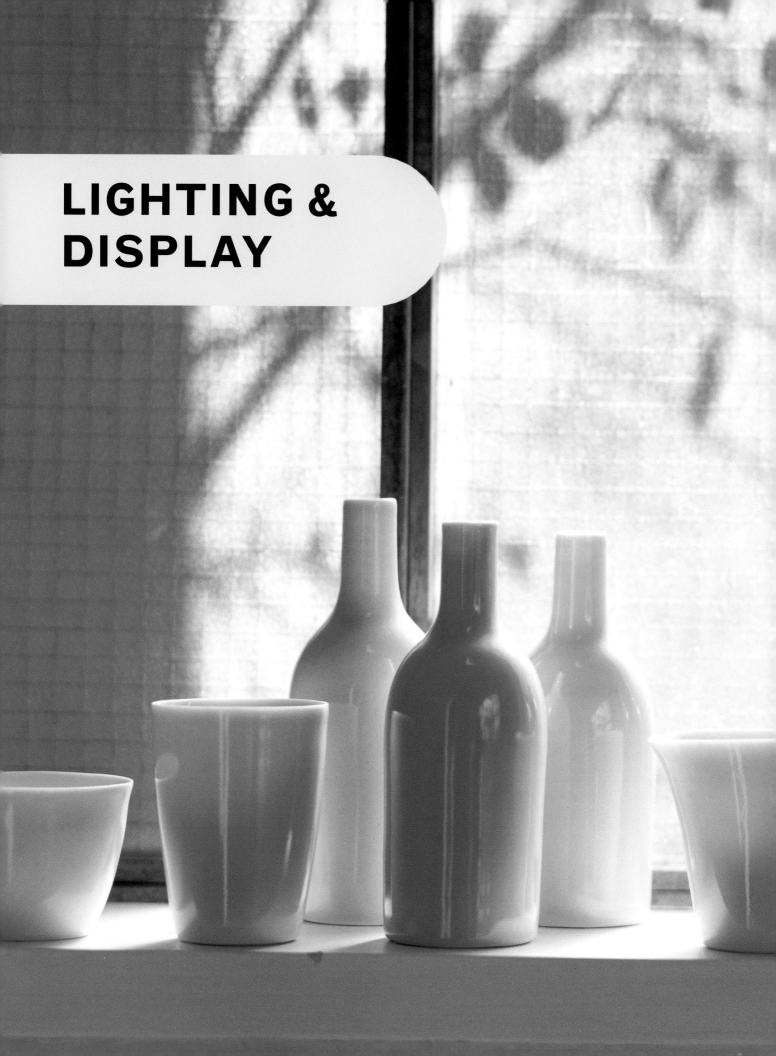

LIGHTING & DISPLAY

LIGHTING & DISPLAY

A modern take on exotic decorating comes together in the provocative display of decorative details. Objects and pictures, flowers and plants, are not so much 'finishing touches' as essential elements that add spirit and joyfulness to the interior. In this context, lighting is also a mood-enhancer, emphasizing what is on view and, at the same time, creating its own decorative impact.

It is important for displays to be meaningful. In the past, exotic cultural artefacts were often collected, at best, like souvenirs and, at worst, like curiosities, with the result that interiors acquired something of the bizarre atmosphere of a museum of social anthropology. More recent versions of ethnic style were similarly cluttered, with every surface, mantelpiece and tabletop laden with its own tribal display. At the other end of the extreme, in early modern interiors, exotic elements were often treated as token imports – the lone carved head standing in for an entire cultural viewpoint.

Flickering candlelight is the perfect form of lighting for an exotic interior. This regular arrangement of night lights in a solid wooden board, combined with the chunky, butter-coloured candles in terracotta bowls, provides an atmospheric display to dine by. Similar holders can be made quite easily from slabs of concrete and chunks of metal.

Neither minimalist nor cluttered, the fusion of modern and exotic elements in display provides an elemental human dimension. There are objects made by hand as expressions of the indomitable creative force, but there are also elements that speak to the senses: decorative light to provide vitality and atmosphere, natural smells and scents to conjure places and moods, sounds that soothe and resonate. The aim is to merge both foreground and background into one holistic environment with an individual flavour all of its own.

Display is less about making a decorative statement and more about making connections. It is not necessary to restrict your choice to artefacts or elements that hail from a single spot on the globe, unless for deep-rooted reasons of affection that is what you really want to do. Neither is it required – although it may be hugely enjoyable – to travel further afield to source the ingredients yourself. Instead, it is essential to pick out items that really appeal to you and express the same basic qualities, whatever their point of origin. An exotic look is a surefire antidote to stay-at-home predictability, and encourages you to examine your surroundings closely.

DECORATIVE LIGHT

Attention should be focused on both the quality of light and the design of the lamp or fitting. The most sympathetic lighting arrangements eschew the hard modern edge of technical fittings such as lighting track and halogen spots; instead the emphasis is on combining many different points of light with the more traditional designs of hanging lanterns, wall sconces, pendant shades and simple lamps – basic types of light that have been in existence for centuries.

Left This strictly duotone room, where black and beige combine in understated elegance, takes its cultural identity from the East. The tasselled paper lanterns, suspended from thin metal poles, are as much decorative as they are functional.

Below Classic but contemporary, Chinese lanterns offer a subdued source of light particularly suited to bedrooms. This low level of lighting renders the saturated red walls even more luminous. The lantern has metal casings at each end to strengthen the shade and give it extra definition.

Right *Decorating with light can be delightfully simple as well as creative. This conical glitter tree is made from a garden topiary frame, with Christmas tree lights threaded over the spirals and chrome baubles placed at regular intervals.*

Below *An integral uplighter, made by attaching a fretwork plaster screen to an existing wall, casts dappled light into an intimate room.*

In living and relaxing areas, light levels should be kept relatively low to enhance the intrinsic mood of relaxation; most homes today are over-bright, which tends to kill atmosphere at the flick of a switch. Under low levels of light, saturated colours become more luminous; neutral schemes less stark. At the same time, many homes also have too few individual light sources, creating a monotonous and somewhat oppressive effect. By contrast, employing multiple light sources will ensure that every area of the space receives a little direct light and so create a series of glowing, intimate focal points that draw the eye to every corner. Placing a number of lights around a room also makes

intriguing contrasts of light and shadow, a pattern that instantly generates atmosphere. If you wish to retain some kind of central hanging fixture, make sure that it is not too bright or the balance of the effect will be lost. Fit discreet dimmer switches to provide flexibility of light level.

Exotic style, so often expressed in colour, comes to life with coloured light. This does not mean the garish effect of coloured lightbulbs, but a gently tinted diffusion created by shading the light source with a coloured shade. Strongly coloured Chinese paper lanterns or pendant shades in organic forms made of wrapped silk, velvet or other types of textile are good solutions; similarly, Moorish-style lanterns, with decorative coloured glazed panels, add richness to a central focus. Glass beads, hung around the base of a simple shade, add a colourful sparkle when backlit.

Patterned light is also very suggestive of an exotic mood. Pierced metalwork shades cast intriguing shadows, either as delicate lacy filigrees or bolder, more graphic shapes; star-shaped-card shades, punched with holes, make an inexpensive alternative. Texture also has a part to play: shades made of hessian (burlap) or a similar homespun fabric or handmade paper have an appealing natural neutrality.

Wall lights that cast at least some of their light onto the surrounding wall surface help to enrich colourful decoration. Small-scale lanterns and metal sconces are in

keeping with the look. Small beaded lamps add the accent of glittery colour dotted around the room. Free-standing paper lanterns, like scaled-down Noguchi lights, provide a soft focus at floor level.

Other suitable floor lights include sculptural organic shapes, such as 'stone' lights, which provide gentle glowing illlumination. For a more theatrical effect, strings of white or coloured fairy lights (Christmas tree lights) can be used to make impromptu effects, outlining a window or doorway, or suspended along the mantelpiece. As these lights emit very little heat, they are safe in close proximity to flammable materials.

Natural light, in the form of flickering candles, lanterns and fires, makes the perfect complement to an exotic look. The dancing patterns of light and shade cast by these mobile sources of illumination add a sense of depth and mystery to both interior and exterior spaces. There is a basic allure to candlelight that is hard to resist, but in hot countries, with doors and windows left open to catch every passing breeze, exposed candles can be blown out in a trice. The answer is to shield the candle in a container of some description. Nightlights placed in jars or glasses are the simplest examples of this idea; more elaborately, hurricane or storm lamps, pierced metal or terracotta lanterns also provide some protection. Lanterns infilled with panels of coloured glass tint the light so that it glows like a jewel, adding another decorative dimension.

Above *Floating candles and glass are a delicate combination that softens even the most unappealing of rooms or settings.*

Left *Nightlight holders massed together always create impact. These hanging lanterns are made from fine chicken wire covered in pieces of perforated paper for a filtered effect that is soothing and sensual.*

VISUAL DELIGHT

Creating an exotic display to suit a contemporary interior is, if anything, too easy. When many products have the lifeless uniformity that comes from mass production, the appeal of anything handmade and idiosyncratic is overwhelming. But it is all too tempting to shop with a certain lack of discrimination, failing to distinguish between objects of real integrity and merit and those that are little more than souvenirs.

It is not always easy to draw the line between tourist trinkets and the genuine article – and there may well be times when the cheerful gaudiness of a souvenir is exactly what is required. In general, however, it is best to avoid those ethnic knick-knacks cynically churned out in their thousands and sold in street markets and airports. Many such items may indeed be handmade, but they often display little true joy or finesse. At the same time, they tend to lack any cultural authenticity; instead, the items being marketed represent a deliberate attempt to play on those clichéd Western misconceptions about what ethnic art is all about. Reputable dealers and importers of exotic artefacts are a better, if more expensive, source; even high street stores with an eye for sympathetic global products are often as good. If you care about maintaining traditional skills and sponsoring local development, steer clear of the tacky mementoes that only debase the artistic currency and serve to line the pockets of marketeers.

Similarly, if you care about originality, bear in mind that the same knick-knacks will be packed in half the suitcases returning from Tangier, Goa or Phuket.

This attitude of discrimination goes hand in hand with a sense of restraint when it comes to creating displays. It is not necessary to restrict your choice to products from a single country or region – but a free-for-all simply won't work. The answer is to exercise a degree of control and combine objects that seem to belong to the same aesthetic family even if they were produced many thousands of miles apart. Too much restraint, however, can result in a visual dead end. One piece of tribal art, no matter how large or dominating, marooned in an otherwise contemporary space is not enough to generate the interesting tension and atmosphere that is a hallmark of the style.

THEMES

Colour provides one obvious common denominator for composing displays. From jewel-like Moroccan tea glasses to Chinese tea tins and brocade-covered boxes, exotic accents of colour entrance the eye. By adding glitter and sparkle, the effect is multiplied: mirror mosaic or twinkling beaded frames, shimmering Banjara wall hangings from Rajasthan encrusted with mirror thread, Mexican tin decorations and cut-crystal doorknobs catch the light and attract the attention.

Texture and form provide another foundation. Hand-thrown African pots, hand-carved wooden trays and platters, chunky silver frames, chased bronze bowls and West African calabashes, their patterns etched with burning sticks, have a rugged simplicity that invites touch and makes a pleasing complement to earthy decoration. Such pieces often work best when they are over-scaled to emphasize their elemental qualities.

Many exotic decorative objects represent a charming fusion of the modern and traditional. In this type of creative recycling, you will find Zulu woven wire bowls made from fine, coloured telephone or plastic-coated, electrical cable, Kenyan aeroplanes and motorcycles fashioned from old

Above   *These Zulu baskets, made from coiled lengths of coloured telephone wire, are a charming example of creative recycling. Baskets like these are as decorative as they are durable and practical; larger versions are often used for displaying fruit and vegetables.*

Left   *An eclectic mix of visual images in a variety of frames on a wall of deep vermilion evokes the embracing warmth of an Indian interior.*

Far left   *Although from disparate parts of the world, these South American cushions, Mexican candle hoods and African carvings have a certain affinity with each other and make a striking and effective display.*

soft-drink or oil cans, and spindly animals, figures and toy machines made from scraps of wire and old bicycle spokes.

Magic and mysticism can also play an important role. The African tribal mask is perhaps the most obvious ritual object, but every culture has its own charms and totems to encourage good fortune and keep marauding evil spirits at bay. Representations of all-seeing eyes (to protect against danger creeping up from behind) are common good-luck charms. Those with a taste for the macabre might be attracted to painted plaster or papier mâché and wire skeleton figures from Mexico and other Day of the Dead ornaments, which provide a satirical commentary on the transience of everyday life. Gods and goddesses are represented in Indonesian shadow puppets – articulated silhouettes made of card and decorated with dull gold – and many Indian postcards, pictures and posters as well as papier mâché figures and ornaments feature the whole pantheon of Hindu deities, from Rama and Shiva to Ganesh, the elephant god. Further east, the Buddha is the focus of spiritual art, carved or cast in wood, brass or bronze, in every size and scale but usually in the characteristic seated pose.

Posters, paint, wrapping paper and all manner of eccentric wallcoverings are only half the story in this kitchen given over to shrine-chic. So exuberant is the decoration that the kitchen appliances seem to fade into the background.

PICTURES

As with decorative objects, many different types of picture can convey the modern exotic fusion. Contemporary art, particularly bold and colourful prints or abstracts, work well where the decoration is equally strong. Black-and-white photography, framed by deep white mounts and black or chrome frames, has a graphic impact in Eastern-style neutral schemes, as does Japanese calligraphy or simple brush-and-ink paintings. Japanese coloured prints, which had such an influence on late nineteenth-century taste, are still widely available as well as affordable. For a touch of kitsch, you could experiment with Indian film posters. With their full-blown graphics and vibrant colours, they certainly add exotic glamour.

Fabric hangings, decorated with shells, mirrors and sequins, feature in many ethnic interiors. The basic quality of the work is an important factor in the success of the final result, as is scale – one large picture will have greater impact than lots of tiny ones.

SITES FOR DISPLAY

Grouping objects tends to increase their decorative impact and underline their visual cohesiveness. This is especially true when pieces are small in scale. In floor-level living, the emphasis shifts downwards and the floor itself becomes a place for display. Large pots, bowls, platters and urns arranged around the hearth or in corners away from main traffic routes provide dramatic focal points. Low shelves and mantelpieces make good places

to display a series of similar objects that can be lined up or arranged in an orderly collection, as well as framed pictures that can be casually propped. Flat-bottomed containers, such as lacquered trays or carved wooden platters, can also be used to collect objects together. Walls, of course, are the obvious site for banner-like hangings and decorative textiles as well as framed calligraphy and photographs. Here, again, a more successful effect can be achieved by displaying a large hanging or a group of pictures rather than a small, lone embroidery or picture with acres of wall space to either side.

For a heightened sense of drama, you can always borrow an idea that features in many different cultures, and display objects in a kind of shrine. Recesses and alcoves housing objects that have some special aesthetic or religious significance occur in interiors around the world. Effectively a three-dimensional frame, a shallow recess in a plastered wall, which is often picked out in a contrasting colour, provides the perfect opportunity to display a beautiful pot or vase, or a collection of household gods. In Japan, niches are used as designated showcases for single objects at a time, providing all the aesthetic contribution in otherwise minimal rooms. In older houses, the alcoves that occur to either side of a chimney breast make natural sites for shrines; alternatively, deep box frames with glass fronts offer a version of the same idea.

Above   *A low, wooden chest acts as a side table and is perfect for displaying this collection of stone vases. The tiger-print upholstery adds to the ethnic feel.*

Right   *Cube-shaped furniture and chunky lampstands are signature pieces of the modern exotic fusion.*

TABLE SETTINGS

Exotic or ethnic-inspired china and glass-ware, serving dishes and place settings pursue the global theme. As with kitchen accessories and equipment, it does help if you enjoy the food and flavours that accompany such designs, many of which reflect a style of eating as well as a type of cuisine. But mixing and matching is also a possibility, both between cultures and with standard Western tableware.

For a minimal Eastern sensibility, you need to focus on the purity of porcelain and lacquerware. In Japan, in particular, the presentation of food is an art in itself, with precisely cut and arranged ingredients making a graphic and orderly display. Bowls tend to take precedence over plates in both Japanese and Chinese styles of eating. Large, white pieces of porcelain or crackle-glaze Japanese noodle bowls, and blue and white Chinese rice bowls, with individual grains of rice making translucent patterns in the china, make very versatile serving or eating dishes. Small lidded dishes and oblong side plates, together with shallow saucers for relishes and condiments, acces-sorize the table; chopsticks elegantly poised on shaped porcelain or lacquer rests com-plete the formal arrangement.

Indian and other types of Southeast Asian food are traditionally eaten with the fingers, scooped up with flat breads or folded into large leaves. Individual small bowls or bamboo baskets, which are often arranged

Zen table settings are coolly understated and undeniably elegant. This simple, red table runner is the key to the look here, where it is offset by the muted colours of the ceramics. The chopsticks placed neatly on the bowl complete the formal arrangement.

on trays, are common methods of serving. Metal tiffin boxes, or Indian portable lunch boxes, make attractive containers.

Ceramic bowls, earthenware casseroles and metal platters complement the long-simmered aromatic flavours of Moroccan cooking, as well as the more robust and spicy Latin American cuisines. Deep indigo glazes set off the citrus shades of fresh lemons and limes; unglazed terracotta dishes make absorbent cooking dishes, becoming sea-soned with repeated use, for meals that are served straight from the oven. Plates are gen-erously sized and boldly decorated with

hand-painted patterns and motifs. Irregular hand-blown coloured tumblers serve to emphasize the ethnic look.

It is important for table coverings to be fairly minimal to complement the china and glassware. They usually take the form of various types of matting rather than full-length cloths. A long runner down the middle of the table creates a decorative cen-trepiece where serving dishes can be arranged. Try split cane or bamboo, woven rush mats or gaily coloured fabric embroi-dered in naive cross-stitch patterns. Place mats share a similar aesthetic.

*A display that is purely
textural tells a story that is
rich in tone, if not in colour.
Mixing harmonious surfaces
so that they play off one
another is a trick that never
fails to please the eye.*

SENSUAL ELEMENTS

Scents, sounds, and living or natural displays have a fundamental role to play in the interior. Smell, the most evocative sense, has the power to transport you to another place, instantly evoking memories of holidays in far-flung exotic locations. Scented candles, room oils and incense, which were once the tell-tale sign of a 'hippy' household, are a modern growth industry and with their increased popularity has come a renewed appreciation of the way in which different scents can operate directly on one's general mood and outlook. Unlike the rather cloying, floral sweetness of many traditional types of pot-pourri, these scents range from appetizing vanilla to sharp citrus tangs, and from spicy cardamom and cloves to deep musk; some are exceptionally complex formulations where a combination of aromas is carefully balanced and blended. Needless to say, there is nothing synthetic or harsh about these scents. Their purpose, unlike that of modern room fresheners or heavily perfumed cleaning products, is not to mask offensive odours or impart a false notion of freshness, but to provide enjoyment and pleasure on the subtlest of all levels. Many such products need to be heated or burned to disperse their scent effectively.

Sound is another evocative element. In hot countries, open doorways that lead onto shaded courtyards, echoing with the soft splash of fountains, provide a literal connection with the outdoor world. Hanging

Restraint rather than richness rules in this scented and tactile display of a single flower in a terracotta pot and a mound of smooth, flat pebbles.

wind chimes by an open window can provide a similar suggestion in areas where indoors and outdoors cannot always be so closely integrated. Chimes come in a variety of materials and designs that make a range of musical noises, from the high tinkling of Chinese brass to the more sonorous bell-like tones of Japanese-style metal chimes or the tocking sound of bamboo.

A more obvious association with the living world comes in the form of plants, flowers and collections of found natural objects. Flower arrangements are often stark and sculptural, featuring tropical and subtropical flowers such as strelitzia, or the bird-of-paradise flower, the thistle-like protea from southern Africa, and various types of orchid. They are best displayed singly or in sparse groups where their rather architectural qualities can be appreciated to the full. Trays of wheat grass, resembling miniature verdant meadows, take the place of the ubiquitous hothouse ferns as indoor greenery. Collections of pebbles or smooth beach stones, or candles stuck in trays of raked gravel or floating among petals in shallow, water-filled bowls, create a Zen-inspired sense of nature in microcosm.

Calico table runner

Combining the vivid hues typical of Central American cottons and woollens with the textile craft qualities of West Africa, this table runner will look distinctive in any setting. Made from calico (heavy muslin) marked out with a freehand design and filled in with fabric paint, it is embellished still further with stamping and sewn-on beads, with the ends fringed to loosen the look.

The calico is folded in half to make the runner thicker and only one side is decorated. The stamp was made from a simple pencil eraser, but you could also sculpt sponges, potatoes or other porous materials to the desired shape. Beads are available in an enormous number of styles and designs.

MATERIALS AND TOOLS

• Length of calico (heavy muslin) • Scissors • Erasable fabric pen • Fabric paint in orange, pink, red and dark purple • 2.5cm (1in) paintbrush • 12mm (½in) paintbrush • Fabric stamp made from a pencil eraser • Lino cutter • Sponge roller • Shimmery sewing thread and needle • Beads

METHOD

First, wash the calico by hand or machine to remove the finish. Leave to dry and then iron. Cut out a piece of fabric that measures double the eventual width of the runner and allows for a generous drop at each end and enough fabric for hemming the side. Fold the fabric in half lengthways and press to show the centre line.

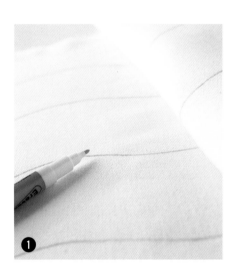

Make your own fabric stamp using a lino cutter to sculpt the desired shape in the pencil eraser. (Rubber stamps are also available in many different designs from craft suppliers.) Apply the purple colour to the stamp with a sponge roller so that the eraser soaks up the paint. Test the stamp on a piece of scrap fabric first, then re-load it and stamp the motif onto the runner at regular intervals over the pink wavy lines, adding more paint to the stamp as you go.

❶ With an erasable fabric pen, draw your design onto one side of the folded calico (the markings will disappear gradually over a couple of days).

❷ Following the fabric pen outlines, apply the orange and pink fabric paints to the calico in wide wavy lines using a 2.5cm (1in) brush, and the red paint as a border with a 12mm (½in) brush. Allow each colour to dry before applying the next.

❸ Once the paint is dry, sew a wavy line of running stitch in shimmery thread to link the centres of the stamp motifs. In the middle of each motif, over the central 'target', sew a series of three beads in toning colours to give punctuation. Insert a stitch between each bead to keep them secure.

Fold the calico outside in and machine stitch the side. Turn the fabric back the right way and, to finish off, fringe each end of the runner by about 12mm (½in).

Knitted cloth lampshade

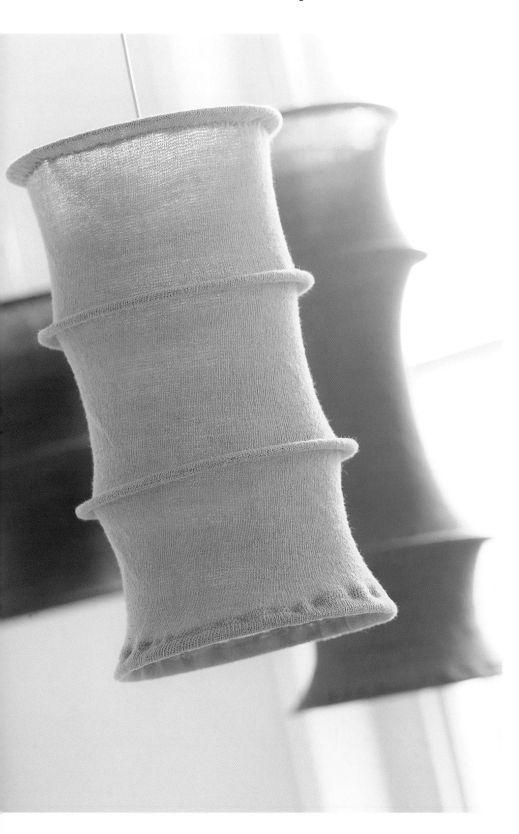

Taking the traditional Chinese paper lantern as a starting point, these lampshades provide instant chic at a fraction of the cost of conventional woven shades. The subtle greens and beiges of the dyed stockinette cloth echo the muted shades of bamboo and will add a complementary splash of colour to a predominantly white decorating scheme.

Lampshade and utility rings (for the light fitting), which are available in diameters up to 48cm (16in), can be bought by mail order through specialist crafts suppliers but are also stocked at certain large department stores. Stockinette, sold at car accessories stores, comes in rolls weighing 250g (8oz), enough to make two 30cm (12in) shades with two lampshade rings. Different shapes of lampshade can be made by varying the size and position of the rings. For reasons of safety, do not use a utility ring with a diameter of less than 15cm (6in). Also, make sure that the lightbulb you use is no brighter than 40 watts.

The instructions given here are for one 30cm (12in) diameter lampshade using two rings (see the olive green shade, right, and in the background of the main picture, left).

MATERIALS AND TOOLS

• Roll of stockinette cloth • Tape measure • Scissors • Fabric dye • 1 utility ring measuring 30cm (12in) in diameter • Sewing thread and pins • 2 plain lampshade rings, measuring 30cm (12in) in diameter • Clothes-pegs (clothespins)

Fold over a seam allowance of 12mm (½in), then pin and stitch the fabric in place (a slight zigzag is best for this type of stretchy fabric). Alternatively, machine stitch to within a fraction of each cross-piece, using the machine foot as a guide against the metal ring to give an even channel.

② To fit the first lampshade ring, it will be easier if you suspend the lampshade from a fixed point. First, pull down the fabric until there is a 17cm (7in) drop all round from the utility ring. Then sandwich the hoop between the fabric.

③ Fit the second lampshade ring at the end of the stockinette as described above, trimming off any excess material and leaving a hem allowance of about 2.5cm (1in). Machine sew using a zigzag setting to neaten the edge. Allow the lampshade to hang, weighted down with a few clothes-pegs, to allow any creases to drop out.

METHOD

First, decide how long you wish the shade to be. Cut the stockinette to twice this length, adding on an extra 12mm (½in) at each ring junction for seams. Dye your complete batch of stockinette according to the manufacturer's instructions and leave to dry.

① Fold the fabric in on itself, from top to bottom, to double the thickness. Take the folded edge and attach it to the utility ring.

Copper wind chimes

The feng shui principles of maintaining good chi, or optimum cosmic currents, often employ wind chimes as a way of promoting harmony in your immediate environment. The ratio of windows to doors in a room is thought to be important in the ancient art of placement. In rooms where windows out-number doors by more than three to one, a wind chime positioned above the door is said to restore the balance and promote harmony. At the very least, this wind chime will bring a soothing sound to your home. It is made from readily available copper tubing and very strong nylon fishing line threaded with glass beads. Different lengths of tubing will vary the pitch of the sound produced.

MATERIALS AND TOOLS

• 6 lengths of 2cm (¾in) diameter copper tubing, pre-cut into 20cm (8in), 25cm (10in) and 30cm (12in) sections • Sandpaper • Wire wool • Brass or copper polish • Soft cloth • Wine cork • Hammer and nails • Pliers • Copper wire, 2mm (¹⁄₁₆in) in diameter, and finer • Nylon mono filament fishing line, 0.2mm (0.0078in) in diameter, strength 2.7kg (6lbs) • Glass beads

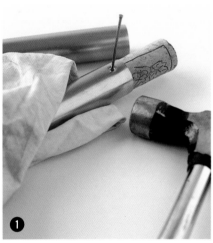

copper from bending inwards, and hammer a short nail into the cork. The nail should be removed with pliers.

2 With the pliers, cut eight lengths of wire, four measuring approximately 35cm (14in) and four 50cm (20in). Curl both ends of all the pieces into a scroll shape with the pliers. Wind finer copper wire around the eight lengths to join them together.

3 Knot and thread the fishing wire through the holes you have made in each copper tube and suspend them from the individual scrolls. You may have to adjust the scrolls slightly with the pliers once all the tubes are in position to make them balance. If you wish to add glass beads to the ends of the tubes for a decorative flourish, you will need to make extra holes in the tubing (see step 1). Finally, hang the chimes with fishing wire from a hook in the ceiling.

METHOD

First, sandpaper the cut ends of the copper tubing. Rub down the length of each tube with wire wool, then polish to a sheen with a soft cloth and brass or copper polish.

1 About 6mm (¼in) down from the top of each tube, make two small holes facing each other. The easiest way to do this is to insert a wine cork in the tube to prevent the

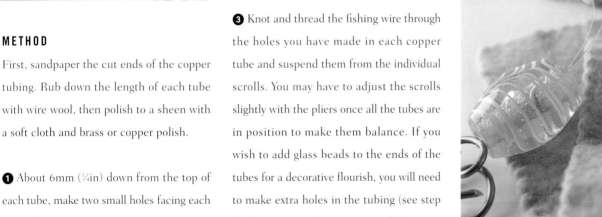

A selective list of stockists

FURNITURE & ACCESSORIES
The Bead Shop
21A Tower Street, London WC2H 9NS
Tel: 0171 240 0931

Emma Bernhardt
301 Portobello Road, London W10 5TE
Tel: 0181 960 2929

Carden Cunietti
83 Westbourne Park Road, London W2 5QH
Tel: 0171 229 8559

David Champion
199 Westbourne Grove, London W11 2SB
Tel: 0171 727 6016

The Conran Shop
Michelin House, 81 Fulham Road, London
SW3 6RD
Tel: 0171 589 7401

The Conran Shop
55 Marylebone High Street, London W1M 3AE
Tel: 0171 723 2223

The Cross
141 Portland Road, London W11 4LR
Tel: 0171 727 6760

Egg
36 Kinnerton Street, London SW1X 8ES
Tel: 0171 235 9315

The General Trading Company
144 Sloane Street, London SW1X 9BL
Tel: 0171 730 0411

Graham & Green
4, 7 & 10 Elgin Crescent, London W11 2JA
Tel: 0171 727 4594

Graham & Green
164 Regents Park Road, London NW1 8XN
Tel: 0171 586 2960

Inventory
26–34 Kensington High Street, London W8 4PF
Tel: 0171 937 2626

Cath Kidston
8 Clarendon Cross, London W11 4AP
Tel: 0171 221 4000

Liberty
214 Regent Street, London W1R 6AH
Tel: 0171 734 1234

Lombok
4 Heathmans Road, London SW6 4TJ
Tel: 0171 736 5171

Muji
Tel: 0171 323 2208 for branches

Neal Street East
5 Neal Street, London WC2H 9PU
Tel: 0171 240 0135

Snap Dragon
247 Fulham Road, London SW3 6HY
Tel: 0171 376 8889

Temptation Alley
361 Portobello Road, London W10 5SA
Tel: 0181 964 2004
(*braid, Indian jewels*)

David Wainwright
61–3 Portobello Road, London W11 3DB
Tel: 0171 727 0707

Wong Singh Jones
253 Portobello Road, London W11 1LR
Tel: 0171 792 2001
(*Indian postcards*)

KITCHENS
Divertimenti
45–7 Wigmore Street, London W1M 9LE
Tel: 0171 935 0689

Divertimenti
139–41 Fulham Road, London SW3 6SD
Tel: 0171 581 8065

Johnny Grey
Fyning Copse, Rogate, Petersfield, Hampshire
GU13 5DH
Tel: 01730 821424
(*designer*)

LIGHTING
Fred Aldous
PO Box 135, 37 Lever Street, Manchester 1
M60 1UX
Tel: 0161 236 2477
(*mail order lampshade fittings*)

Christopher Wray Lighting
Tel: 0171 736 8434 for branches

John Cullen Lighting
585 King's Road, London SW6 2EH
Tel: 0171 371 5400

FABRICS
Designers Guild
269–77 King's Road, London SW3 5EN
Tel: 0171 351 5775

Pierre Frey
251 Fulham Road, London SW3 6HY
Tel: 0171 376 5599

Habitat
Tel: 0845 6010740 for branches

Ikea
Tel: 0181 208 5600 for branches

John Lewis
Tel: 0171 629 7711 for branches

HARD FLOORING
Paris Ceramics
583 King's Road, London SW6 2EH
Tel: 0171 371 7778

Wickes DIY
Tel: 0500 300 328 for branches

CARPETS & RUGS
David Black
96 Portland Road, London W11 4LN
Tel: 0171 727 2566

Christopher Farr Rugs
212 Westbourne Grove, London W11 2RH
Tel: 0171 916 7690

Fired Earth
Twyford Mill, Oxford Road, Adderbury,
Oxfordshire OX17 3HP
Tel: 01295 812088
(*mail order*)

Roger Oates Design
The Long Barn, Eastnor, Ledbury, Herefordshire
HR8 1EL
Tel: 01531 631611

Roger Oates Design
1 Munro Terrace, Cheyne Walk, London
SW10 0DL
Tel: 0171 351 2288

The Rug Company
124 Holland Park Avenue, London W11 4UE
Tel: 0171 792 3245
Tel: 0171 467 0690 for catalogue

Rugstore
637 Fulham Road, London SW6 5UQ
Tel: 0171 610 9800

Helen Yardley
A–Z Studios, 3–5 Hardwidge Street, London
SE1 3SY
Tel: 0171 403 7114
(*designer of contemporary rugs*)

NATURAL FIBRE FLOORING
The Alternative Flooring Company
14 Anton Trading Estate, Andover, Hampshire
SP10 2NJ
Tel: 01264 335111

Crucial Trading Ltd
79 Westbourne Park Road, London W2 5QH
Tel: 0171 221 9000

WINDOW TREATMENTS
The House of Shutters
Tel: 0171 610 4624 for brochure

Jali
Albion Works, Church Lane, Barham, Near
Canterbury, Kent CT4 6QS
Tel: 01227 831710
(*decorative edging*)

Scumble Goosie
Lewiston Mill, Toadsmoor Road, Stroud,
Gloucestershire GL5 2TB
Tel: 01453 731305
(*MDF screens*)

TILES
Fired Earth
(*see under Carpets & Rugs*)

World's End Tiles
Silverthorne Road, London SW8 3HE
Tel: 0171 819 2100

PAINTS
Auro Organic Paints (GB) Ltd
Unit 1 Goldstones Farm, Ashdon, Near Saffron
Walden, Essex CB10 2LZ
Tel: 01799 584888

Brats
281 King's Road, London SW3 5EW
Tel: 0171 351 7674

ICI Dulux
Tel: 01753 550555 for stockists

Farrow & Ball
Uddens Estate, Wimborne, Dorset BH21 7NL
Tel: 01202 876141 for stockists

Grand Illusions
2–4 Crown Road, St Margarets, Middlesex
TW1 3EE
Tel: 0181 744 1046

Paint Library
5 Elystan Street, London SW3 3NT
Tel: 0171 823 7755

Paint Magic
Tel: 0181 960 9960 for branches and stockists

Paintworks
5 Elgin Crescent, London W11 2JA
Tel: 0171 792 8012

Papers and Paints
4 Park Walk, London SW10 0AD
Tel: 0171 352 8628

The Stencil Store
Tel: 01923 285577 for mail order and stockists

The publisher would like to thank Richard Conn for his help with special photography; Cathy Sinker, David Coote, Anjie Davison, Susie Ross and Claire Cousins for making projects; Philippe Boucry, Fred Collin and David Coote and Atlanta Bartlett for the use of their homes as locations; Paintworks, 5 Elgin Crescent, London W11 2JA (0171 792 8012) for supplying paints; Jali Ltd, Albion Works, Church Lane, Barham, Near Canterbury, Kent CT4 6QS (01227 831710) for decorative edge trims; J Crispin & Sons, 92–6 Curtain Road, London EC2A 3AA (0171 739 4857) for veneer; Margaret Doyle for proof-reading, and David Lee for the index.

The publisher also thanks the following photographers and organizations for their kind permission to reproduce the photographs in this book.

1 Christian Sarramon; 2 Alexander van Berge; 4 David George/Homes & Gardens/Robert Harding Syndication; 5 above Louis Gouillard/Sty: Choubet Soulagtol/Marie Claire Idées; 5 centre Luc Wauman; 5 below Alexander van Berge; 6 Gilles de Chabaneix/Sty: Catherine de Chabaniex/Marie Claire Maison; 8 Sergio Dorantes/IMPACT; 8–9 Nicolas Bruant/Homes & Gardens/Robert Harding Syndication; 9 Ben Edwards/IMPACT; 10 above Mads Mogensen; 10 below & 11 Alexander van Berge; 12 Christian Sarramon; 12–13 Alexander van Berge; 13 Christian Sarramon; 14 Ray Main; 15 above & below Christian Sarramon; 16 above Ray Main; 16 below Henry Wilson/The Interior Archive; 17 Vincent Thibert/Agence Speranza; 18 Verne Fotografie; 18–19 Verne Fotografie(Raymond Jacqueryns); 20 & 21 above Christian Sarramon; 21 below Gilles de Chabaneix/Sty: Catherine Ardouin/Marie Claire Maison; 22 above Charles Coates/IMPACT; 22 below Mads Mogensen; 23 Alexander van Berge; 24 Verne Fotografie (Bataille & Ibens); 25 Ray Main; 26 Marie Claire Maison/Marie–Pierre Morel/Sty: C. Puech; 26–7 Christian Sarramon; 27 Simon Upton/The Interior Archive; 28 Gruner & Jahr; 28 above Silvio Posada/Leticia Marin/La Casa de Marie Claire/Gruner & Jahr; 29 Roland Beaufre/Agence Top; 30–1 Vincent Thibert; 32 Deidi von Schaewen; 33 Louis Gaillard/Sty: Chombart/Soulaytol/Marie Claire Idées; 34 Ray Main; 35 Alexander van Berge; 36 Giovanna Piemonti; 37 Alexander van Berge; 44–5 Ray Main; 46 & 47 Christian Sarramon; 48 & 49 Ray Main; 50 Pieter Estersohn/LachaPelle (Representation); 51 Cecilia Innes/The Interior Archive; 52–3 Deidi von Schaewen; 53 Ray Main; 54 Christian Sarramon; 54–6 Giovanna Piemonti; 57 left Mark Luscombe-Whyte; 57 right Ray Main; 58 above Tim Beddow/The Interior Archive; 58 below Christian Sarramon; 59 Giovanna Piemonti; 62–3 Cecilia Innes/The Interior Archive; 68 Cecilia Innes/The Interior Archive; 70 Nicolas Bruant/Homes & Gardens/Robert Harding Syndication; 71 above Christophe Bluntzer/IMPACT; 71 below Christian Sarramon; 72 Henry Wilson/The Interior Archive; 72–3 Deidi von Schaewen; 74–5 Andrew Wood/The Interior Archive; 75 Camera Press; 76 Christian Sarramon; 77 Tim Beddow/The Interior Archive; 78 Alexander van Berge; 78–9 Ray Main; 79 Deidi von Schaewen; 80 Andrew Wood (Des: Osborne & Little)/The Interior Archive; 81 left Christian Sarramon; 81 right Alexander van Berge; 82 Gilles de Chabaneix/Sty: Catherine de Chabaneix/Marie Claire Idées; 83 Vogue Living; 84 left Vogue Living; 84 right Christian Sarramon; 85 Roland Beaufre (Maison Tanger)/Agence Top; 87 Ray Main; 92 Andrew Wood/The Interior Archive; 94 Luke White/Axiom Photographic Agency; 95 Ray Main; 96 Andrew Wood/The Interior Archive; 96–7 Alexander van Berge; 97 Caroline Arber/Homes & Gardens/Robert Harding Syndication; 98 Camera Press; 99 Jim Holmes/Axiom Photographic Agency; 100 Gilles de Chabaneix/Sty: C. Ardouin/Marie Claire Maison; 101 Paul Ryan (Des: Scott Bromley)/International Interiors; 102 Andrew Wood/The Interior Archive; 103 Petrina Tinslay/Belle Magazine; 104 Jim Holmes/Axiom Photographic Agency; 104–5 Marie Pierre Morel/Sty: C Ardouin/Marie Claire Maison; 105 Nicolas Bruant/Homes & Gardens/Robert Harding Syndication; 106 Luc Wauman; 107 Andrew Wood/The Interior Archive; 108 Eric Morin/World of Interiors; 108–9 Mads Mogensen; 109 Christian Sarramon; 110 & 111 Gilles de Chabaneix/Sty: C. Ardouin/Marie Claire Maison; 112 Christian Sarramon; 113 Andrew Wood/The Interior Archive; 120–1 Earl Carter/Belle Magazine; 122 Simon Kenny/Belle Magazine; 123 above & below Ray Main; 124 above Marie Pierre Morel/Sty: Bayle/Puech/Marie Claire Maison; 124 below Christian Sarramon; 124–5 Marie Pierre Morel/Sty: M.Bayle/C.Puech/Marie Claire Maison; 125 Marie Pierre Morel/Sty: Bayle/Puech/Marie Claire Maison; 126 & 127 above Ray Main; 127 below & 128 Henry Wilson/The Interior Archive; 129 left Ray Main; 129 right Marie Pierre Morel/Sty: Bayle/PuechMarie Claire Maison; 129 below Gilles de Chabaniex/Sty: C. Ardouin/Marie Claire Maison; 130 above Andrew Wood/The Interior Archive; 130 below Ray Main; 131 Tom Leighton/Ikea room; 132 Alexander van Berge; 133 Andrew Wood/The Interior Archive; 140 above Andrew Wood/The Interior Archive; 140 centre Marie Pierre Morle/Sty: Bayle/Soulrier/Marie Claire Maison; 140 below Giovanna Piemonti; 141 above Andrew Wood (Osborne & Little)/The Interior Archive; 141 centre Santi Caleca; 141 below Verne Fotografie (Bataille & Ibens).

Every effort has been made to trace the copyright holders, architects and designers. We apologize in advance for any unintentional omission and would be pleased to insert the appropriate acknowledgment in any subsequent edition.

The photographs on the following pages were taken especially for Conran Octopus by Verity Welstead: 38–43, 64–7, 88–91, 114–19, 134–9